Cream City Chronicles

WHi Image ID 9524

Publication of this book was made possible in part by grants from

Gary and Anne Grunau

The Harry F. and Mary Franke Idea Fund
of the Greater Milwaukee Foundation

Wisconsin Preservation Fund

Daniel Hoan Foundation

Dorothy Inbusch Foundation

D.C. Everest Fellowship Fund

Cream City Chronicles
Stories of Milwaukee's Past

John Gurda

Wisconsin Historical Society Press

Published by the
Wisconsin Historical Society Press

www.wisconsinhistory.org

Photographs identified with PH, WHi, or WHS are from the Society's collections;
address inquiries about such photos to the Visual Materials Archivist
at the above address.

Cover: Panoramic View of Milwaukee, WHi Image ID 12022
Back cover: Author photo by Christopher Winter

Printed in the United States of America
Cover designed by Ryan Scheife/Mayfly Design
Text design by Marilyn Barr, Dedicated Business Services

27 26 25 24 23   3 4 5 6 7

Library of Congress Cataloging-in-Publication Data
Gurda, John.
   Cream City chronicles : stories of Milwaukee's past / John Gurda.
      p. cm.
   Compilation of the author's columns originally published in the Milwaukee journal.
   Includes bibliographical references and index.
   ISBN: 978-0-87020-375-6 (hardcover : alk. paper)
   ISBN: 978-0-87020-758-7 (pbk. : alk. paper)
   1. Milwaukee (Wis.)—History—Anecdotes. 2. Milwaukee (Wis.)—Social life and
customs—Anecdotes. I. Title.
   F589.M657G86 2007
   977.5'95—dc22
                           2006017100

⊗ The paper used in this publication meets the minimum requirements of the American National Standard for Information Sciences—Permanence of Paper for Printed
Library Materials, ANSI Z39.48-1992.

To the memory of Frank Zeidler (1912–2006)—
mayor, mentor, and model Milwaukeean

Contents

❧

Contents

A Heritage of Diversity

Water: The City's Lifeblood

The Flush of Success
Alterra Coffee and Sewerage District Brew an

Summer

Making a Living

A Sense of Place

Fall

The Common Good

Contents

Celebrations!

Contents

Milwaukee's downtown, 1901

Introduction
History as Story

I was in fifth grade the first time I heard, or rather saw, history defined. Sister Josetta, one of the more formidable spirits at St. Mary's School in Hales Corners, wrote "history" on the chalkboard, paused to see if the class was paying attention, and then deftly altered the word to make it "his/story." The study of the past, she declared, was the story of man.

Sister Josetta was missing more than half the population, of course —some later scholars would insist on "her/story"—but the point she made was valid: History is, above all, story. Too often presented as a life-less catalog of dates and events, presidents and kings, history is in fact a rich chronicle of human experience that, wherever you start, has a beginning, a middle, and any number of ends, including the present.

Cream City Chronicles is a book of history as stories. They had their first incarnation as columns in Milwaukee's Sunday newspaper, beginning with the *Milwaukee Journal* in 1994. The *Journal*'s editors were launching a feature called "Our Town," and they invited me to write about the city's history. My first column, a short piece describing the old Falk brewery, appeared on March 6, 1994. Barely a year later, the afternoon *Journal* and the morning *Sentinel* merged to form, natu-rally, the *Milwaukee Journal Sentinel*. "Our Town" didn't survive the move, but the history column did, and it's been appearing in the Cross-roads section of the *Journal Sentinel* ever since, on the first Sunday of each month.

Writing for the newspaper meant following in the footsteps of columnists like Bill Hooker, Russell Austin, Robert Wells, Jay Joslyn, Jay Scriba, and others who looked back to Milwaukee's roots on a regular basis. Some of those figures, particularly Scriba, were heroes of mine, and I felt both honored and a bit intimidated to be carrying on their tradition. At the same time, my goal for the column was crystal-clear: to connect what was happening in the present with what had happened in the past. That meant supplying the historical context for the newest landmark, the latest ethnic shift, or the freshest scandal, most often descriptively but also, when the occasion called for it, critically. The columns became a sort of running historical commentary on the passing scene. One unintended consequence was that some began to seem dated only months after they were published. All have been revised for this book, some substantially, in an effort to make them "evergreen" for a new (or returning) round of readers.

However well-read and however well-written, newspapers commonly end up wrapping fish or lining litter boxes. I'm grateful that the Wisconsin Historical Society has seen fit to rescue these stories from such an ignominious end. I'm also pleased that *Cream City Chronicles* will become, as Sister Josetta might have said, part of our permanent record, taking whatever place it may find in the distinguished roster of Society publications going back to the state's formative years.

My own approach to history is unabashedly presentist. I have the utmost respect for those who study Phoenician trade routes or colonial American handcrafts, but my interest centers on how we got *here*, to this time and place. And so history, in these pages, is Milwaukee's story—his and hers and ours and theirs. Wherever we reside, the story of the community around us can provide a lively context for our personal stories. But history has even more to offer. An awareness of the past can foster qualities all too rare in the swelling tumult of the twenty-first century: insight, a sense of proportion, and hope for the journey ahead. May *Cream City Chronicles* be an agreeable companion as the story—and the journey—continue.

John Gurda

Spring

Milwaukee, 1858

Solomon Juneau

Josette Juneau

Solomon Loves Josette

Frontier Valentines Found
Happiness in Milwaukee

Their romance began in the wilderness. He was a French-Canadian voyageur who had been knocking around the Great Lakes region for almost a decade. She was a fur trader's daughter, French and Menominee by ancestry, who had probably never set foot outside Wisconsin. When they met, Milwaukee was not even a dot on the map, but Solomon Juneau and Josette Vieau became the first sweethearts in the city's recorded history.

Josette's father, Jacques Vieau, had been trading with local Indians since 1795, when he opened a small post overlooking the Menomonee Valley in today's Mitchell Park. Vieau and his wife, Madeline, had at least twelve children, and their brood spent part of each year in Milwaukee. Josette was one of the oldest.

A newcomer entered the household in 1818, when Vieau brought Solomon Juneau to Milwaukee as his clerk. After what must have been a closely watched courtship, given the family's cramped quarters, Solomon and Josette were married in 1820. He was twenty-seven—practically middle-aged at the time—and she was seventeen.

The newlyweds spent their first years together at other Vieau posts in southern Wisconsin, but they were back in Milwaukee by 1825. Solomon went into business for himself, opening a trading post at the present intersection of Water Street and Wisconsin Avenue. Perched on the first dependably dry ground above the mouth of the Milwaukee River, it soon became the busiest post in the region.

Although they left no trail of love letters, the Juneaus were, by all accounts, devoted to each other. The most tangible sign of their bond was Josette's seventeen pregnancies. Thirteen of her children survived infancy, materially increasing the population of the frontier outpost.

The Juneau family's lives changed dramatically in the 1830s, when eastern speculators arrived with dreams of building a city on the swamp that covered central Milwaukee. Solomon quickly moved from furs to real estate as his stock in trade. In partnership with Morgan Martin, a well-connected Green Bay lawyer, he became the impresario of Milwaukee's east side, serving as promoter, postmaster, and developer.

Mrs. Juneau kept a lower profile, but she was a full participant in local affairs. In addition to raising her own kids, she acted as hostess, nurse, and midwife for the growing number of women in the settlement, virtually none of whom spoke the French she used at home. Josette was also Milwaukee's guardian angel on one memorable occasion in 1835. While her husband was away on business, she patrolled the primitive streets all night to ward off a threatened Indian uprising.

Although they had little in common with the Yankees who were swarming over Milwaukee, the Juneaus were popular figures in the settlement. Morgan Martin remembered Josette as "a most amiable and excellent woman." Another contemporary praised her "calm and stoical self-possession" and "great, hearty and beautiful goodness." Solomon himself was described as "one of Nature's noblemen" and an "unselfish, confiding, open-hearted, genial, honest and polite" individual who deserved remembrance as a "primal civic hero." In 1846, when Milwaukee received its city charter, voters paid Juneau the compliment of electing him their first mayor.

The adulation of their new neighbors must have been gratifying, but the Juneaus, after so many years in the wilderness, eventually grew tired of the city springing to life around them. In 1848, they moved out to Dodge County and founded a settlement called Theresa, in honor of Solomon's mother. Solomon opened a grist mill and general store there for aspiring farmers, both Yankee and German, who were settling in the vicinity, but he also continued to do business with bands of Indians who still roamed the territory.

The Juneaus' rural idyll ended in 1855, when Josette died at the age of fifty-two. Although he stayed in business, Solomon was reportedly devastated by the loss. He died less than a year later, during a visit to the Menominee reservation in northern Wisconsin.

A simple stone marks the couple's grave in Calvary Cemetery today. It is seldom visited, except by history buffs and the occasional relative, but the tombstone stands as a lasting monument to wilderness romance. In a time notably devoid of hearts and flowers, Solomon and Josette offered living proof that love can abide.

Milwaukee, 1850

Elijah Loves Zebiah

Pioneer Sweethearts Gave
Romance an Early Start

We don't usually think of our ancestors as romantics. If their photographs are any clue, Wisconsin's early settlers were a generally cheerless lot doomed to lives of unending work and unbending morals. The faces in a thousand old tintypes look as if they had scant time for the softer sentiments.

The pictures are deceptive. The sober expressions of the 1800s were the inevitable result of long camera exposures and a different attitude toward presentation. The camera-eating grins we wear today say, in effect, "Like me." The stern faces of our ancestors said, "Respect me."

Appearances to the contrary, love did flourish on the frontier. The pioneers were never immune to sentiment, and some could be downright mushy on occasion. Consider Elijah Estes. Born in North Carolina in 1814, he decided to seek his fortunes in the West at the age of twenty. Lacking a horse, he walked most of the thousand miles to Chicago, arriving footsore and broke. There he met a dark-haired young woman named Zebiah Wentworth, whose family was already prominent in the embryonic city. The couple fell in love and pledged, over the course of a long winter, to spend the rest of their lives together.

Elijah apparently found Chicago too settled for his tastes. As soon as the snow had melted, he walked north to a wilderness outpost he knew only as "Milwaky." On April 5, 1835, months before the inaugural land sale, Elijah sent Zebiah what might have been Milwaukee's first love letter. "Mine Own and Beloved," the missive began, "Your last prayer has kept ringing in my ears like music of comfort and my gloomy way was made bright."

The hike from Chicago had taken three days, and Elijah had been forced to contend with cold rain and marauding Indians along the way. "But when I think of you," he sighed, "the sunshine comes, and I forget I am chilled and hungry." Things had begun to look up as soon as he reached Milwaukee. After buying an ax, food, and a blanket (all on credit), Estes claimed a half-mile of lakeshore land in the vicinity of today's South Shore Park.

The young lover finally allowed himself to dream. Elijah described for his fiancee the home he was going to build, a snug cabin with a fieldstone fireplace and a front yard filled with "nothing but flowers, tall flowers—zinnias, hollyhocks and dahlias." Those dreams were tempered by frontier realities:

> I am fearful that it may be hard for you at first, the change from comfort to almost Indian life, but I know that your love for me will bear you through. Fortunes always smile on those who love and who loves more dearly than we? I am thinking all the time of what you told me when you said farewell and I am going to make the chips fly from this new ax, to finish the cabin and come back for you. I wish there was some little token that I might send you, but I can find nothing, although I still hope to by my next. But you and I need no tokens, for our token is the memory of the pledge. O, what a charm its memory will ever work over us; a memory dearer than the riches, man's hoard of wealth. Any one can get their jot of gold, but even the tiniest shred of golden memory is far beyond the measure of mere money.
>
> If it had not been for you, I would have gone back home to North Carolina as soon as I set foot in Chicago, although lame from my thousand mile walk. But when we met, I knew that my fate was sealed and happily to labor for you in your northern land. The days are lonely without you, but I am coming for you soon.

Elijah Estes was as good as his word. After "proving up" his claim, he returned to Chicago, married Zebiah, and brought her north to the cabin he had built overlooking the lake. The marriage was a resounding success. Elijah and Zebiah Estes became prosperous farmers, raising six children to adulthood and building a fifteen-room brick mansion at what is now the corner of Shore Drive and Estes Street. The home was a Bay View showplace until 1922, when it was torn down to make way for South Shore Park.

The Estes family also did well in real estate. When a massive iron mill opened on Bay View's lakefront in 1868, their farm was suddenly a few blocks south of Milwaukee's largest industry, and houses began to spring up in fields once filled with hay and wheat. When the village of Bay View was incorporated in 1879, Elijah became a pillar of the community, serving as a charter trustee and library board member. He also tried, without success, to stop Bay View's merger into Milwaukee eight years later. "Though I glory in Milwaukee," said the old settler, "having lived here and seen her grow up from a wilderness into a metropolis, I do not glory in her enough to pay her taxes."

It was perhaps his last public statement. Elijah and Zebiah died within a few months of each other in 1887, he at seventy-three and she at seventy-seven. Milwaukee's pioneer valentines now rest in Lake Cemetery, a little-visited burial ground in St. Francis. Carved on their plain stone marker is a fitting epitaph: "For so He giveth His beloved sleep."

The Early Years

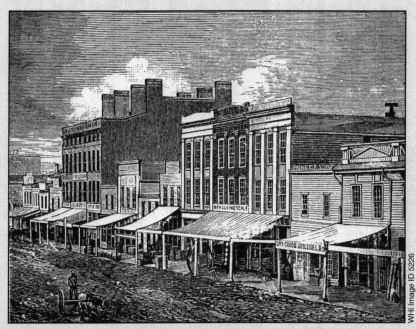

West Side of East Water Street, Milwaukee, 1844

WHi Image ID 5226

Layton House

From Indian Fields to Forest Home
South Side Corner Has Seen It All

Local history is all about layers. Distinct waves of settlement rise and fall, one after another, each leaving traces of its presence to mingle with all that follow. The result, over time, is a series of layers, physical and cultural, that give our oldest places their distinctive blends of old and new. The past, however altered, is always present.

One of Milwaukee's oldest places is the intersection of Lincoln and Forest Home Avenues. The South Side crossing doesn't look particularly historic. A used-car lot, a Walgreen's, and a window shop crowd the main corners, and a chain-link fence marks the edge of Forest Home Cemetery to the south. The intersection seems unremarkable, but looks are deceptive: The Lincoln-Forest Home area has more layers than a Bavarian torte.

The first took shape at least a thousand years ago. While Europe was mired in its Dark Ages, local Indian tribes were building hundreds of effigy mounds in what is now Milwaukee County. The greatest number—more than sixty in all—were clustered on the South Side, within a one-mile radius of Lincoln and Forest Home. Most were simple cones, but the mounds included panther effigies nearly 250 feet long.

Later arrivals planted corn around the mounds, but not cornfields as we know them. When the Potawatomi and allied tribes moved to Milwaukee in the 1600s, they cleared the woodlands around our intersection and heaped up hundreds of corn hills, each perhaps a foot high and three or four feet wide. The native plantings ultimately covered nearly a square mile of land, and the chief of the local village was named, naturally, Cornstalk.

Indian Fields, as the first white settlers called the area, was both the major mound site and the largest "farm" in native Milwaukee. It was also the scene of the natives' last stand. In 1838, when the United States evicted the last of the local tribes, hundreds of Potawatomi and their neighbors gathered at Indian Fields for the long, sad journey to reservations west of the Mississippi.

The Yankee settlers who came in their wake proceeded to methodically wipe out every trace of the native presence. Beginning in the late 1830s, they leveled the mounds and plowed up the corn hills until even the memories were erased. Dozens of Indian skulls plundered from the effigy mounds ended up as curios in the collections of pioneer farmers. The pioneers soon added layers of their own to the local landscape. In 1848, they began work on the Janesville Plank Road—today's Forest Home Avenue. The road quickly became the main-traveled highway to all points southwest of Milwaukee, and it helped open the area to new settlers.

Two of the plank road's more prominent residents were John and Frederick Layton, a pair of Englishmen, father and son, who purchased the narrow triangle of land between Lincoln and Forest Home east of S. Thirty-first Street. The Laytons owned a downtown meat market, and their South Side acreage served as a pasture for beef cattle. John and Frederick were quick to take advantage of their position on the plank road. In 1849, they opened the Layton House, a sizable hotel that served wayfarers heading into Milwaukee from the countryside. For the grand sum of six bits (about seventy-five cents), the weary traveler received a room, two meals, a glass of whiskey, and a morning cigar—as well as a stall and hay for his oxen.

The Laytons were soon too busy to run a hotel. They leased the inn to full-time managers and devoted their attention to the meat-packing business, a field that would make Frederick one of the wealthiest men in Milwaukee. The hotel went out of business in the early 1900s, but the building, amazingly, is still with us. Carved up into apartments today, the Layton House is a nondescript cube of Cream City brick looming behind a former fur store at 2504 W. Forest Home Ave.

The hotel's original neighbors were some of the quietest in Wisconsin. In 1850, St. Paul's Episcopal Church, a well-heeled Yankee congregation, purchased seventy-three wooded acres across the plank road from the Layton House. Surveyed and subdivided into tiny lots, the land became Forest Home Cemetery, which quickly emerged as Milwaukee's premier burial ground. Its more prominent "residents" included John and Frederick Layton; the meatpackers' final resting place lies barely a block from their old inn.

It was not until the early 1900s that the city finally caught up with Forest Home. A wave of blue-collar ethnics, nearly all of them Polish or German, surged out from the South Side's older neighborhoods, covering the area with modest but well-kept cottages, duplexes, and Polish flats. They called the neighborhood Layton Park, and many of their descendants are still living in the community today.

From the vanished earthworks of the mound-builders to the imposing headstones of Forest Home's departed millionaires, from the rural comforts of the Layton House to the urban congestion of a blue-collar ethnic enclave, the Layton Park area has witnessed change on the grand scale. Today, particularly in the melancholy cool of autumn, it's easy to feel the weight of the accumulated layers, easy to sense an older presence. Are there ghosts? None I've met but, in the breadth and depth of the area's history, there is evidence of a force nearly as impressive: the transforming power of time.

Byron Kilbourn

Flawed Founder
Byron Kilbourn Had a Cast-Iron Conscience

It was, in a sense, the return of the native. In 1998, after 128 years in the sandy soil of northern Florida, Byron Kilbourn's body was replanted in the hard clay of Forest Home Cemetery. The transfer marked the return of a founding father to the scene of his greatest endeavors. It also marked Kilbourn's return to the scene of the crime.

A number of history buffs met Byron face to face in the days before the 1998 ceremony, and I mean that literally. His coffin was a bullet-shaped, cast iron beauty that weighed half a ton, but its most surprising feature was a glass window concealed beneath an iron plate. The staff at Brett Funeral Home—Byron's temporary resting place—slid the plate aside for visitors to reveal an early example of the embalmer's art. Although the glass was obscured by mildew and moisture, you could easily make out Kilbourn's mummified face, upper dentures, red chin whiskers, bow tie, and frock coat. Such an intimate encounter with such a legendary figure felt awe-inspiring, macabre, and a little sacrilegious all at the same time.

The reburial ceremony at City Hall involved simpler emotions. Speaker after speaker extolled Byron Kilbourn as "a great man," "a visionary," and even "a philanthropist," a civic giant to whom the current generation of Milwaukeeans owes an enormous debt.

It was all true enough. The Connecticut-born Yankee was a man of vision, intelligence, and boundless determination, and no one did more to put Milwaukee on the map. His entire career was a succession of firsts. In 1836, Kilbourn launched Milwaukee's first newspaper, the aptly named *Advertiser*. In 1843, he built the first dam across the Milwaukee River at North Avenue and a mile of canal below it. The canal became a millrace that provided power for Milwaukee's first industrial district. In 1847, Kilbourn organized Wisconsin's first railroad, the Milwaukee & Waukesha. Steam trains, he declared, would give his city "a larger business than can be commanded by any other western town, Chicago not excepted." Kilbourn also made time for public office, serving as Milwaukee's mayor in 1848 and again in 1854.

Byron Kilbourn was a force on the frontier, but let's make no mistake: His chief object in life was Byron Kilbourn. He was determined to make his settlement on the west bank of the river the heart of Milwaukee, and he pursued that goal with a competitive zeal that verged on nastiness. In 1835, for openers, he refused the offer of a full partnership with Solomon Juneau, founder of the East Side, preferring to develop his own lots and lay out his own street network. The result, more than 160 years later, is a string of downtown bridges that cross the river at an angle.

Kilbourn was even less pleasant to George Walker, the South Side's founder. In 1836, the West Side's impresario built a bridge across the Menomonee Valley at Second Street, diverting traffic to his own settlement and giving Walker's Point, as he put it, "a cooler." In promoting his own townsite, Kilbourn acted as if his rivals didn't exist. He operated a steam launch that ferried passengers from lake ships into town—if they agreed to land on the West Side—and in 1836 he published a map of the "City of Milwaukee" that left the East Side entirely blank.

This civic partisan played his most memorable role as a leading instigator of Milwaukee's Bridge War. Kilbourn contended that West Siders had the right to chop off their end of any bridge that crossed from the East Side. On the night of May 7, 1845, that's exactly what they did, touching off a wave of comic-opera violence that gave Milwaukee a short-lived reputation for lawlessness.

Although he was a terrible neighbor, Byron Kilbourn saved his most creative acts of competitive skullduggery for the railroad business. In 1852, he tried to gain sole control of Wisconsin's pioneer line by issuing fraudulent stock to friendly parties. His fellow directors reacted by firing him. Not to worry. Kilbourn soon founded another railroad, the La Crosse & Milwaukee, and aimed it toward the Mississippi on a more northerly route. It was in connection with the La Crosse line that Kilbourn showed his true ethical colors. In 1856, hoping to secure a land grant from the state legislature, he distributed nearly

$800,000 in railroad securities to Wisconsin officials, editors, and business leaders.

Kilbourn was blessed with a cast-iron conscience; he saw absolutely nothing wrong with his actions. When asked why, in his opinion, Wisconsin's governor had taken a gift of $50,000 in bonds, Kilbourn's explanation was simple: "I believe he accepted it for the reason that he thought the company could well afford to make such a donation without doing it any material damage, while to him the sum was large enough to confer a real benefit."

The would-be railroad czar won the land grant but lost his good name. In the investigation that followed, Wisconsin was exposed as a cesspool of corruption, and the promoter's public career came to a rather inglorious end. Kilbourn finished his days in Nixonesque isolation, moving first to Hot Springs, Arkansas, and then to Jacksonville, Florida. It was there that he died on December 16, 1870, and it was there his body remained until 1998, when Frank Matusinec and Historic Milwaukee, Inc. brought it back to the city he had helped to found.

Time has a way of restoring tarnished reputations. Crooks become "characters," and their misdeeds are seen as "colorful." That's certainly true in Kilbourn's case, but let's give the entrepreneur his due. It was through his efforts, particularly on behalf of railroads, that Milwaukee rose from obscurity to become a regional powerhouse. Whatever his ethical shortcomings, Kilbourn's career illustrates a truth we've known all along: It's not always the nice guys who finish first.

Increase Lapham Examining a Meteorite, 1869

Lapham's Legacy

Pioneer Scientist Casts a Long Shadow

Most Wisconsin pioneers had other things to occupy their time: felling trees, plowing up prairies, planting crops, and building their first homes. Even in those first, tentative days of settlement, there was one newcomer who looked beyond the workaday necessities to the mysteries of the world around him: Increase Allen Lapham. It was Lapham who brought the spirit of scientific inquiry to Wisconsin. More than a century after his death, this Renaissance man remains one of the most compelling figures in the state's history.

Like many of Wisconsin's pioneers, Lapham was a native of upstate New York. His father was a Quaker contractor who worked on the Erie Canal, and that canal provided young Lapham with a practical apprenticeship in surveying, stone-cutting, and civil engineering. He put his new skills to work on canal projects under way in Kentucky and Ohio. It was in Kentucky that Lapham wrote his first scientific paper, a treatise on the geology of the Louisville area that was published in a national journal. The author was all of sixteen years old.

In 1836, after several years of work on Ohio canals, the self-taught prodigy moved to Milwaukee. Lapham's patron and employer was Byron Kilbourn, who had once been his boss in Ohio. Kilbourn was the guiding light of Milwaukee's West Side, and his pet project was a canal linking his settlement with the Rock River. Lapham was hired as the canal's chief engineer, at a salary of $1,000 a year.

Kilbourn and Lapham were Milwaukee's original odd couple. Byron Kilbourn's ethical lapses were legendary, and his competitive instincts bordered on the ruthless. Lapham, by contrast, was ever the earnest Quaker, a non-combative sort described by one admiring contemporary as "a modest, retiring, industrious, excellent man." Despite their sharp differences in taste and temperament, the two men were lifelong friends. Lapham ultimately served as executor of Kilbourn's considerable estate.

The Rock River canal project came to nothing, but Lapham decided to stay in Milwaukee, patching together a livelihood as a real estate agent, mapmaker, surveyor, engineer, and even landscape architect. One of the New Yorker's larger projects was the preliminary layout of Forest Home Cemetery.

Gainful employment (and some judicious land purchases) gave Lapham just enough time and money to continue his scientific career. In 1838, only two years after his arrival, he prepared a catalogue of all the plants and shells in the Milwaukee area. Lapham went on to publish a guide to Wisconsin that found a ready market among prospective immigrants. Other studies explored topics as diverse as lunar tides on Lake Michigan, grasses of the Midwest, the geology of Wisconsin, and North American meteorites.

One of Lapham's studies has shown particular staying power: *The Antiquities of Wisconsin*. Published by the Smithsonian Institution in 1855 and reprinted by the University of Wisconsin Press in 2001, the book describes every known Indian mound in the state, complete with drawings in Lapham's own meticulous hand. Wisconsin was the world center of effigy mound culture, and Lapham's book is the major record of a civilization whose works were usually plowed under or paved over as soon as white settlers arrived.

Increase Lapham also ranks as Wisconsin's first environmentalist. In 1867, when most of the state was still a wilderness, Lapham warned that it would become a biological desert if the reckless clear-cutting of its forests continued. Arguing from both economic and ecological grounds, he urged the conservation of existing forests and the planting of new ones. Later Wisconsinites like John Muir and Aldo Leopold would carry the thread of Lapham's argument in new directions.

The forest report demonstrated Lapham's fervent belief in applied science. Another project carried that belief even further. Lapham had long been in love with weather. He had been charting temperatures and barometric pressures since his teenage years, and he became convinced that weather could be predicted. Since the prevailing winds carry storms from west to east in North America, he reasoned, why not use telegraph wires to warn everyone downwind of approaching danger?

Years of assiduous lobbying by Lapham and others finally led to the creation of the U.S. Weather Service in 1870.

His scientific achievements were obvious, but Increase Lapham was a model citizen as well as a model scholar. He volunteered his services as register of land claims in frontier Milwaukee. He was a founder of the Wisconsin Historical Society, an early member of the Milwaukee School Board, and a loyal supporter of the Milwaukee Female Seminary, later Milwaukee-Downer College.

In 1875, after nearly four decades of tireless activity, Lapham retired to his farm on the shores of Oconomowoc Lake. Even in retirement, he made systematic measurements of the lake's depths and temperatures for an essay on the cultivation of fish. On September 14, at the autumnal age of sixty-four, Lapham suffered a fatal heart attack while rowing on the lake. He died as he had lived: in the presence of nature.

Few Wisconsinites have ever approached Lapham's stature as a citizen scholar, and his example has continuing significance. Instead of focusing on a narrow specialty, Increase Lapham fearlessly tackled subjects as disparate as mounds, meteorites, and meteorology. He pursued science for the oldest and purest reason of all: for the love of it.

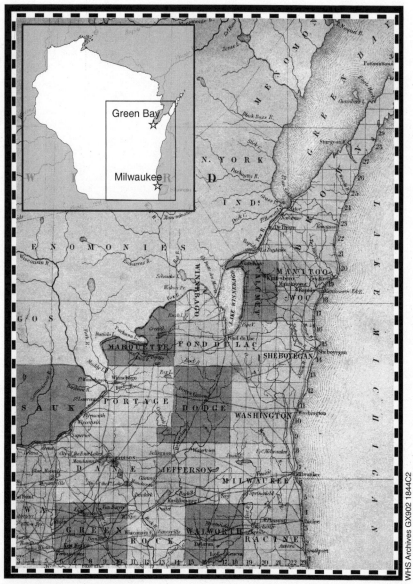

Map of Wisconsin, 1844

To Green Bay the Long Way
Pioneers Would Have Missed the Kickoff

The road from Milwaukee to Green Bay is one of Wisconsin's busiest. Some motorists head north to gamble or shop, but the real crush occurs whenever the Packers play a home game. Since 1994, when the team stopped playing part of its Wisconsin schedule at County Stadium, the Milwaukee faithful have flocked to Titletown for their fix of green and gold. Nearly everyone travels north on either Interstate 43 or Highway 41. Both roads are nearly as wide as football fields, with four traffic lanes, generous shoulders, and rest stops the size of parks. The journey takes about ninety minutes if you speed, considerably more in game-day traffic.

The trip is nothing special today, but moving that fast would have been beyond imagining for an earlier generation of Milwaukeeans—nearly as fanciful as traveling at the speed of light for us. Few measures of progress—or change, at least—are more graphic than the acceleration of the journey to Green Bay in the last 200 years.

Green Bay, not Milwaukee, was Wisconsin's metropolis two centuries ago. At a time when the only "packers" in town carried bundles of beaver pelts on their backs, "La Baye" was a regional center of the French-American fur trade. A network of Indian trails connected the settlement to every corner of Wisconsin, including Milwaukee.

With the coming of permanent white settlers in the 1830s, the Milwaukee-Green Bay route took on new importance. As a seat of government and the location of the land office, Green Bay was a regular stop for Milwaukee's pioneers. Impatient with Indian trails, they hacked a new road through the virgin forest along the present corridor of Fond du Lac Avenue and Highway 175.

It was Increase Lapham who left the most complete account of the trip to Green Bay in the mid-1800s. A surveyor by trade and a scientist by instinct, Lapham was a Wisconsin original. Arriving in 1836, he became the resident expert on the future state's plants, shells, grasses, rocks, and Indian mounds.

Early one winter morning in 1843, Lapham hitched a cutter to his favorite horse, Adelaide, and headed north. He carried with him a supply of "overcoats, cloaks, and furs sufficient for a winter exposure at the North Pole," all provided by a thoughtful wife. Lapham was courting frostbite in a one-horse open sleigh, but the cold weather was actually an advantage. Heavy snows and freezing temperatures had turned much of the road into "a very smooth and hard track . . . over which we glided swiftly and easily." The same highway was nearly impassable in the luxuriant mud of spring.

The sojourner encountered sleet at the edge of town (then N. Twenty-seventh Street), suffering "a kind of sting which can only be compared to the bite of a mosquito." As the sleet softened to snow, Lapham unfurled his umbrella, finding it "a very useful article." Signs of civilization were thinning out by the time he crossed the present county line near Menomonee Falls. The highway had been cleared not long before, and Lapham had to watch carefully "to avoid striking the stumps and logs that are very close to the road." By midday, our traveler had crossed the belt of "hilly and very broken country" we know today as the Kettle Moraine. Signs of Indian occupation multiplied near Theresa: wigwams, maple-sugaring houses, and a pair of native women by the roadside.

After traveling from dawn to dusk, horse and driver finally stopped for the night at "the famous village of Fond du Lac, which consists of two houses, one a blacksmith shop!" Lapham's host was Mason Darling, whose evening guests included a chief who had taken part in the massacre of American settlers at Chicago during the War of 1812. His name was Saugun, or "He Who Scares Everybody."

Lapham kept a more leisurely pace on his second day, following the military road along the eastern shore of Lake Winnebago. The day's sights included Indian mounds, sledges loaded with limestone, and the bustling village of Taycheedah, a crossroads settlement considerably larger than Fond du Lac. Lapham spent the night at a home in Brother-town, an unusual community of thoroughly Westernized Native Americans who had migrated from New York State. Before turning in, he attended a "very correct and appropriate" prayer service that lasted until eleven p.m.

The Milwaukeean was on his way by eight the next morning. "The weather clear and cold," he wrote, "I needed all my furs." Lapham hit the Fox River near Kaukauna and followed it all the way into Green Bay. By nightfall, he had arrived at the Astor House, the settlement's finest hotel. Lapham found the town "very dull," with "little business," but he noted with approval that Green Bay had started both a lyceum and a temperance society.

A trip we can now complete in two hours of smooth driving took Increase Lapham three days of occasionally rough sledding. The journey we make in heated steel cocoons, listening to the music of our choice, is the same one he finished with nothing but the winter sky overhead and his own thoughts for company. Although we still find plenty to complain about, it's obvious that we've conquered both distance and the physical challenges of travel.

Few of us would willingly go back to 1843, but I wonder if we haven't numbed our palates in the process, if we haven't drained our encounters with the world around us of their singular power. A man of remarkable curiosity, Increase Lapham traveled "solitary and alone," alert to every shift in the outer landscape he crossed and the inner landscape he carried with him. "To a person of contemplative mind," Lapham wrote, "this is by far the most agreeable way of traveling. The mind then has free scope to wander at random or to pursue certain courses of thought . . . to such objects as most particularly interest us."

How many Milwaukeeans, hurtling along the road to Green Bay on game day, ever pause to take advantage of the same opportunity?

Watertown, 1842

Taking Their Toll
Pay-to-Drive Roads Have Been Tried Before

Tolls? In Wisconsin? The very idea seems so completely foreign, so utterly . . . Illinois. For the last fifty years, motorists have been paying through the nose to drive through New Jersey, Pennsylvania, Ohio, Indiana, and Chicago. The highway robbery finally stops at the border of Wisconsin, where the ways are truly free. Tolls may be a political hard sell, but they surface with surprising regularity whenever the state's transportation future is discussed. At a time when freeways are wearing out and funds to replace them are scarce, why not charge people for the privilege of driving?

The idea, in truth, has been tried before. In the 1840s, long before minivans and semitrailers, most Wisconsinites traveled by horse and buggy—or ox and wagon. The "roads" they endured were the stuff of nightmares. Most were little more than crude trails slashed through the virgin forest, riddled with stumps and punctuated with sinkholes. Edward Holton, a pioneer capitalist, described Wisconsin's early roads succinctly: "They were at best bad enough, and at times almost impassable." Conditions were worst in spring and fall, when wet spells turned even the best roads into wagon-eating quagmires. For a city on the grow, the seasonal gumbo was intolerable. Milwaukee depended absolutely on its commerce with Wisconsin's farmers—especially in wheat —and that commerce was too often bogged down in a sea of mud.

Plank roads were the answer, declared a growing chorus of promoters. Well-known to settlers from back East, the roads were basically overgrown wooden sidewalks constructed of oak planks, perhaps eight feet long and three inches thick, set on stringers anchored in the earth. Why not try them in Wisconsin? An epidemic of plank-road fever was soon sweeping the state. Between 1846 and 1871, the legislature chartered no fewer than 135 plank road and turnpike companies. All were private firms authorized to charge tolls on roads constructed with private funds.

One of the first, and easily the most successful, was the Watertown Plank Road. Work began on the Milwaukee end of the turnpike in 1848, and the local press couldn't have been happier. "Plank roads defy the weather," wrote the *Milwaukee Sentinel.* "Let us not rest, till we have them." The newspaper urged every citizen to support the Watertown venture: "No better or safer investment can be had, or more productive in Wisconsin, than the stock of this road."

The fifty-eight-mile stretch to Watertown was completed in 1853. A journey that had taken three or four days during the rainy seasons now required a day and a half in any season, and teamsters could pull twice the weight they had in earlier years. They paid a one-way toll of sixty-six cents for the privilege—about $16 in current dollars—but no one seemed to mind. "We maintain," wrote the *Sentinel*, "that an ample off-set to this tax will be found in the saving of feed, whip, lashes, horse shoes and broken wagons."

By 1860, toll roads radiated outward from Milwaukee like spokes in a wheel, most of them planked, all of them privately owned. The roads generally followed diagonal paths to the destinations they were named for: Green Bay, Appleton, Fond du Lac, Lisbon, Wauwatosa, Watertown, Janesville, and Muskego. Those corridors are still very much in use today, and most still bear their original names, from Green Bay Avenue to Janesville Road. Wherever you encounter a diagonal street slicing through Milwaukee's rectangular grid, chances are that it was a pioneer plank road.

The heyday of planked highways was short-lived. In order to save wear and tear on tender hooves, no nails were used in their construction; the planks were simply tamped into the earth with heavy mauls and left to settle. The boards were free to float away in downpours, which they did with distressing frequency, and those that didn't wander off tended to rot after a few years.

Competition from a different mode of transportation sounded the real death-knell for plank roads. Milwaukee's first railroad made its maiden run to Waukesha in 1851, and before long, the state was criss-crossed with rail lines. As freight and passenger traffic left the plank roads for the railroads, most companies slashed their maintenance budgets. In 1863, the *Milwaukee Sentinel* pronounced the once-proud Watertown Plank Road "an unmitigated nuisance." The section nearest Milwaukee, reported the paper, was "in a wretched condition, broken and dilapidated in the last degree." One by one, as the companies behind them dissolved or defaulted, the toll roads became free public highways.

Could the situation be reversed? Could Wisconsin return to a system of privately funded toll roads? The idea has a certain appeal. Government would be off the hook for construction and maintenance costs, and motorists would have to pay for a system they actually used, just as bus riders pay for mass transit. But the concept also runs counter to a long-held and widely shared public expectation, one created, in part, by the demise of the plank roads themselves. Decades before the rise of the private automobile, Wisconsinites came to believe that public roads are a public right, free for all and free for all time. Consider this 1873 act of civil disobedience described by the *Milwaukee Sentinel*:

> Last Friday [July 18] a number of milkmen and gardeners assembled and marched to a toll gate off the Green Bay road and with ax, pick and shovel, hacked, picked and shoveled the structure out of existence. They then warned the keeper to remove his office beyond the city line "quick as he could" and allowed him forty-eight hours to accomplish the work. The belligerents had long expressed disatisfaction with the collection of mileage within the city limits, and thus summarily disposed of the matter.

Pay-to-drive partisans need not know for whom the bell of public opposition tolls. It tolls for them.

Early Electrical Switchboard, ca. 1882

Unplugged

Periodic Blackouts Force a Return to the Distant Past

It happens more often than the power companies would like to admit. A lightning bolt strikes, a piece of equipment fails, or a hapless squirrel chews through a live wire and—wham!—it's the nineteenth century again. The current might return in a few minutes or a few hours, but blackouts, while they last, give us a sharp taste of the darkness our ancestors took for granted. All the complicated wiring in our walls, all the expensive gizmos on our counters and floors are absolutely useless.

The experience, in my opinion, isn't all bad. I have particularly vivid memories of a summer-evening blackout in our Bay View neighborhood a few years ago. The first thing we noticed was the silence. Without the hum of the refrigerator, the whir of the fan, or the strains of Lyle Lovett on the stereo, the house was utterly, eerily quiet. It was strange enough that the kids were gone for at least a few hours. With the power off, our home was as still as a tomb.

My wife, Sonja, suggested walking the dog, a somewhat befuddled Bichon named Elmo, down to the lakefront. The same idea had occurred to a few hundred other residents; I had no clue that there were so many canines in Bay View. Those without pooches sat on their porches, watching the parade and talking with neighbors. Candles were burning, flashlights at the ready.

After surprising a deer on our way through St. Francis Seminary (Elmo didn't notice), we walked north toward South Shore Park. A knot of friends had already gathered on the lake bluff there. We sat with them for perhaps half an hour, trading jokes and telling stories, as dragonflies clacked in the air above us and lights came on in the buildings across the bay. Our neighborhood was separated from Milwaukee's shimmering downtown by more than space. Bay View seemed, for the moment, like an anachronism, a throwback to pre-settlement times.

It was hard to believe, as darkness fell, that Milwaukeeans had once resisted the coming of the light. Between 1881 and 1885, the city's aldermen either rejected or crippled no fewer than eight applications for electric lighting franchises. Ignorance was not the problem. A number of breweries, beer gardens, hotels, and stores had already installed private systems, and local residents were familiar with the "artificial suns" of the electric age. But attempts to shed light on a wider public met with repeated failure.

The problem was politics. Since 1852, the Milwaukee Gas Light Company had enjoyed the exclusive right to light the city's streets. By the early 1880s, the system included 90 miles of gas mains and more than 2,000 streetlamps. Electricity was an obvious threat, and gas company lobbyists swarmed to City Hall whenever a new franchise applicant appeared. Electric power, they charged, was untested, expensive, and a grave threat to public safety.

It was not until 1885 that the logjam was broken. In late November, a Chicagoan with the unlikely name of S.S. Badger secured a franchise from a suddenly pliant Common Council. In a related development, the Council's president, John Hinsey, became a part-owner of Badger Illuminating.

As the Badger system grew, electricity lost its novelty. By 1888, the *Milwaukee Sentinel* could report that electric lamps were "becoming general for street illumination." "We must have them," declared the paper, "because the electric light seems to be the measure of the enterprise of a community." The only group inconvenienced by the new system, according to the *Sentinel,* was servant girls, "whose good-night squeeze at the gate has all the romance knocked out of it in the white light of the electric lamp."

Milwaukee has been all lit up ever since—with the exception of nights like the one in Bay View a few years back. As Elmo pulled us up Delaware Avenue in the dark, Sonja remarked that people probably knew each other better in the days before TVs and air conditioners sucked them all inside. Given the number of porch-sitters and strollers we passed, it was hard to disagree.

The lights finally came back on at about eleven, four hours after they went out. The gears meshed in sequence again, the background noises all returned, and the entire neighborhood pulsed with the blinking of "12:00" in practically every room. Was I sorry to see it end? A little.

Blackouts, like blizzards, always bring a sense of emancipation from routine, a serendipitous release into an alternate reality. I wouldn't choose a regular diet of darkness, but it's good, once in a while, to go without. It's useful to return, however briefly, to the world of our ancestors, if only to keep ourselves from taking the wonders of the present for granted.

Questions of comparison are inevitable. Our ancestors' world was simpler and smaller than ours, of course, but does that make it better, worse, or simply different? I would argue for different. A night in accidental darkness means a face-to-face encounter with the ambiguity that seems to drive the modern age. Technology, you realize, always complicates as well as liberates, and every gain involves a loss. Electricity gives us independence—from darkness, from drudgery—and at the same time takes our independence away; we need its power as much as we need food and water. It is humbling, when the lights go out, to remember that the welfare of our entire society hangs by a single thread made of copper and humming with electrons.

A Heritage of Diversity

WHi Image ID 2280

Milwaukee, ca.1909

Lucien H. Palmer, 1907

Black Power, Milwaukee-Style
African-American Political Tradition Has Deep Roots

At some point in the not-too-distant future, Milwaukee will elect a black mayor. The prospect might seem a bit ironic in a town generally known for beer, brats, and bowling, but it will hardly be revolutionary. When an African American takes the city's highest office, he or she will represent the culmination of trends, both demographic and political, that have been gathering force for decades.

Milwaukee's black political tradition is actually older than the city itself. In 1835, at the beginning of urban time in the upper Midwest, an African American named Joe Oliver voted in Milwaukee's very first election. Only free white males were legally eligible, but conditions were fluid on the frontier. The men of the community—all thirty-nine of them—decided that "all the actual settlers" should vote, and that included Oliver, who worked as Solomon Juneau's cook.

It would be more than thirty years before the next black ballot was cast. An 1849 state referendum on "Negro suffrage" produced ambiguous results, but blacks were denied the vote in practice. That changed in 1865, when Ezekiel Gillespie, a railway porter and community leader, sued Milwaukee's election commissioners. In 1866, the Wisconsin Supreme Court ruled that the 1849 referendum had, in fact, granted Negro suffrage, and African Americans have been voting ever since.

Winning elections was another matter. Grinding poverty, growing prejudice, and a minuscule population were towering obstacles to success at the polls. Until the 1920s, African Americans made up less than one percent of Milwaukee's population—hardly a power base for any aspiring politician.

That makes Lucien Palmer's victory all the more surprising. Born into slavery in Alabama, Palmer moved to Milwaukee in 1878 and worked variously in catering, real estate, and insurance. In 1906, he became the city's first African American to hold office, winning a seat in the State Assembly. Although he was a prominent citizen and political activist, Palmer's victory was, in part, a case of mistaken identity; voters apparently confused him with a white politician named Palmer.

The Great Migration of the Teens and Twenties put black political hopes on more solid footing. No party had the group's undivided allegiance. Some African Americans voted Republican—the original party of liberation—while others favored Socialist, Progressive, or Democratic candidates. In the 1930s, when Franklin Roosevelt's New Deal softened the harshest blows of the Depression, African Americans moved as a body into the Democratic camp.

It was in the 1930s that blacks became regular contenders for office, a trend supported by their growing concentration on the city's North Side. Joe Trotter, whose *Black Milwaukee* is the standard source on the community's formative years, describes the contests of the period. In 1936, attorney James Dorsey narrowly lost the Sixth Ward aldermanic race to Samuel Soref, the white incumbent. Cleveland Colbert came even closer in the 1942 Assembly election, losing only after his opponent demanded a recount. In 1944, finally, LeRoy Simmons, a real estate and insurance agent, won a seat in the State Assembly. Simmons, a Democrat, prevailed in part because of a split between Republicans and Progressives.

With the community's dramatic growth after World War II, electoral success was assured. African Americans soared from 1.5 percent of the city's population in 1940 to 15 percent in 1970, and blacks became a familiar presence in Milwaukee's public life. Isaac Coggs won an Assembly seat in 1952, launching a political dynasty that's still going strong. Born in Muskogee, Oklahoma, Coggs was an accountant who earned his degree from the University of Wisconsin. In 1964, after six terms in the Assembly, he moved to a seat on the County Board. In 1956, Vel Phillips, a Milwaukee-born attorney, became the first African American (and first woman) to serve on the Common Council—her initial step in a storied public career.

Other pioneers of the 1950s and 1960s included Cecil Brown (Assembly, 1954), Walton Stewart (Assembly, 1956), Raymond Lathan (Assembly, 1964), Lloyd Barbee (Assembly, 1964), Calvin Moody

(County Board, 1964), Orville Pitts (Common Council, 1968), and Clinton Rose (County Board, 1968).

As the years passed, black political influence expanded from the ward level to the world beyond the North Side. Monroe Swan moved up to the State Senate in 1972. Lloyd Barbee became a pivotal figure in the effort to desegregate Milwaukee's schools. In 1978, after several years in the judiciary, Vel Phillips became the first African American to win statewide office, serving as Wisconsin's secretary of state.

Ben Johnson, who followed Phillips as alderman, became the Common Council's first African-American president in 1976. (He also served brief periods as acting mayor when Henry Maier was out of town.) Seven years later, Richard Artison took over the Milwaukee County Sheriff's Department. In 1996, Artison became the first African American to contend seriously for the mayor's seat, winning 40 percent of the vote against John Norquist.

The struggle has never been easy, but an African-American political tradition is well-established in Milwaukee. The 2004 elections marked a turning point. In a city whose population was 37 percent black, five of the ten mayoral candidates were African Americans, and one of them, Common Council President Marvin Pratt, narrowly lost to Tom Barrett. Five months later, Gwen Moore, an energetic state senator, scored a decisive victory in the race to represent the Milwaukee area in Congress.

Does that mean that Milwaukee—and America—have moved beyond the black-white divide, that we can finally judge our candidates on the content of their characters rather than the color of their skin? The answer is "No"; you'd have to be blind to ignore the racial factor in any election. But we're closer, much closer than we were.

South Sixteenth Street, Milwaukee, ca. 1940

Street of Many Nations

Chavez Drive Gives a New Face to Milwaukee's Historic Diversity

Sometimes a single street can tell a city's story. Take, for instance, Cesar Chavez Drive, a thoroughfare most Milwaukeeans probably still identify as S. Sixteenth Street. For the last 150 years, its history has mirrored, on the level of everyday life, the sweeping changes in the community around it.

A visit to the street is especially revealing in the light of recent demographic trends. In the late 1990s, Milwaukee became a majority minority city; Americans of African, Latino, Asian, and native heritage now outnumber those of European background. No other street marks that shift more clearly than Cesar Chavez Drive.

My personal history intersects with the street at more than one point. My father, a genetically frugal South Sider, did all the grocery shopping in our family, and Sixteenth Street was part of our Saturday-morning rounds. I have clear memories from the 1950s of pinching bananas at Jahr's, buying meat at Harlfinger's, and standing in the stately lobby of the Wisconsin State Bank.

The new Southgate was already luring customers away, but Sixteenth Street, in those days, was a prosperous shopping center in its own right, lined from National Avenue to Greenfield Avenue with grocery stores, bakeries, butcher shops, bars, and stores selling everything from locks to accordions. City directories of the 1950s reveal a lingering European presence in the merchants' names—German, primarily, but also Polish, Scandinavian, and Slovenian.

Fifteen years later and fresh out of college, I returned to Sixteenth Street as a staff member of Journey House, a youth center housed in the old Patterson Drug Store. Many of the familiar landmarks were still there, including such stand-bys as the Sanitary Comforter Company, the Saratoga Club, and the street clock outside Jensen Jewelry. (It was the last in the city, and now graces the front of the Milwaukee Public Museum.) Much was familiar, but the street was less prosperous in the

43

early 1970s than I remembered it from childhood. As older families departed for new neighborhoods and new shopping centers, the street had begun to struggle economically. Several storefronts on Sixteenth were vacant, and some had been taken over by social service agencies like ours.

There had also been a pronounced shift in the area's population. The families served by Journey House included a scattering of Latinos, but the greatest number were blue-collar households with roots in rural Wisconsin. The parents on our resident council came from Two Rivers, Cascade, Sturgeon Bay, and several other out-state communities. In one of the great undocumented migrations in Wisconsin's history, thousands of rural families had come to the metropolis in search of industrial jobs, and the area around Sixteenth Street was one of their strongholds.

Fast-forward to the twenty-first century. The embryonic Latino community of the early 1970s has grown to maturity, and the scene along Cesar Chavez Drive—a name adopted in 1996—resembles something you'd find in Juarez or Tijuana. In the four blocks between National and Greenfield, you can buy sombreros and cowboy boots, mangos and cactus pads, paletas and piñatas, and a full assortment of Spanish-language videos and CDs. There are no fewer than seven Latino restaurants on Chavez Drive, most of them Mexican but one (the Playa Café) serving take-out Puerto Rican food.

My favorite business on the street is Mercado El Rey, which features a grocery store, a butcher shop, a video store, a bakery, a restaurant, and even a dry goods store under the same roof. I'm a lunchtime regular at the market's taqueria, and I often bring home gingerbread pigs and churros from the bakery. It's useful, I think, for anyone with white skin to feel like a minority on a regular basis, and El Rey is one of the most interesting places to do it.

Although the street's Spanish accent is most pronounced, that is by no means the whole story. There is an Asian supermarket on Chavez Drive owned by a Hmong family, and a substantial number of Anglo businesses are still thriving. In the residential areas east and west of the street, you'll encounter practically anyone: Latinos, Southeast Asians, a variety of whites, and African Americans. When open-housing advocates marched down Sixteenth Street behind James Groppi in 1967, local residents stoned them. A generation later, open housing is an accomplished fact.

Diversity, in other words, is the neighborhood's hallmark today, and in that sense, the community has returned to its oldest traditions. Those traditions are preserved most faithfully in the area's churches. The near South Side has one of the greatest concentrations of nineteenth-century church buildings in the Midwest, if not the entire country. Their steeples spike the skyline east of Chavez Drive, providing a view from I-94 that is one of the most picturesque, and most characteristic, in Milwaukee.

What the steeples demonstrate is the polyglot character of the near South Side as it developed. Each group built its own churches: German, Irish, Czech, Yankee, Norwegian and, somewhat later, Slovenian and Ukrainian. Local Lutherans put up two churches in the same block of Scott Street between Eighth and Ninth—one for Germans and one for Norwegians. The various groups met and mingled on the neighborhood's commercial streets. English was once a minority language on Sixteenth Street. Today, on Chavez Drive, it is once again.

The story told by Cesar Chavez Drive, in all its incarnations, is a classic urban story, one that conveys an elementary lesson: Cities are constantly in motion and nothing in them remains still for long. But the neighborhood's history also offers an insight specific to Milwaukee: diversity is our birthright. In 1850, only four years after the city was chartered, immigrants and their children made up nearly two-thirds of the population. In the late 1800s, Milwaukee was the most "foreign" city in the country. In the early years of a new century, ethnic heritage remains the focus of some of the most varied and most vibrant festivals on the continent.

For all our vaunted conservatism, there has always been a cosmopolitan edge to life in this city. Although the process has never occurred without conflict, Milwaukee has long been a place where the world's currents meet. The diversity revealed in the current landscape is, in some respects, an updated and amplified expression of our most important character trait.

The danger, of course, is that older groups will resist, if only in their hearts, what they perceive as the encroachment of uninvited newcomers. That tack was tried in earlier periods—by Yankees looking with distrust at recently arrived Germans, then Germans at Poles, Poles at Latinos, and whites at blacks, to name just a few. The only possible result is an anxious separatism. Far better, I think, to acknowledge the fact that we have all been newcomers at one time or another. Far better to accept Milwaukee's growing diversity as a vital part of the American story, a story that continues to astonish and enrich.

Class differences persist and racism will not die, but the pageant goes on. For those who would learn, the world is at Milwaukee's doorstep.

Young man at his Bar mitzvah, 1910

Highlighting Hebrew Heritage
Jewish Community Is Well-Established in Milwaukee

They were never Milwaukee's largest ethnic group. The neighborhoods that were once theirs have long since become havens for other newcomers. Even the old places of worship have been either torn down or handed down, but Milwaukee's Jewish community remains one of the area's most vibrant. Internally diverse and fully engaged in civic life, its members have had a deep and enduring influence on the life of the larger community.

The first Jews arrived even before Milwaukee became a city. Rabbi Louis Swichkow published a masterful account of local Judaism, *The History of the Jews in Milwaukee*, in 1963, and his story begins with the pioneers of the 1840s. By 1856, a decade after the city's incorporation, there were nearly 200 Jewish families in town—and three synagogues.

Most of the newcomers were from the German states of Europe, and many considered themselves Germans who happened to be Jews, not unlike German Catholics or German Lutherans. Jewish immigrants took full part in the Turner movement, mutual aid societies, and German theater and singing groups, helping to build Milwaukee's reputation as the "German Athens of America." Rabbi Elias Eppstein underlined the point in 1873: "We are Germans by tongue; Germans by will of reasoning our way onwards; . . . Germans by the desire to seek knowledge and wisdom, and foster them; Germans by uniting in social life; and Germans by assisting each other in times of need."

The emergence of the Jews as a distinct ethnic group took place somewhat later in the century, and it reflected a shift in the sources of immigration. By the late 1800s, legions of Jews were fleeing poverty and persecution in eastern Europe, particularly in Russia. Milwaukee's Jewish population soared from perhaps 2,000 in 1875 to 8,000 in 1900, and the majority were newcomers.

There were distinct, and sometimes painful, differences between the old and the new immigrants. Many German Jews were entrepreneurs who had done quite well in the New World. Some of their eastern

European brethren arrived with little more than the clothes on their backs. The Germans also gravitated to the Reform movement in Judaism, while the eastern Europeans were more uniformly Orthodox. At least seven synagogues, all Orthodox, emerged in the crowded immigrant quarter of the near North Side before 1906.

Despite some initial reluctance, the earlier arrivals reached across the cultural divide and extended a helping hand to the newcomers. In 1900, they established the Milwaukee Jewish Settlement and began to offer a full range of services from a building on N. Fifth Street. The Jewish Settlement's programs included cooking classes led by the legendary Lizzie Kander. In 1901, Mrs. Kander collected her recipes in one handy volume and called it *The Settlement Cookbook*. Two million copies later, it remains a staple in America's kitchens.

The Settlement's patrons probably included a young Russian girl named Goldie Mabowehz. She arrived in 1906, when she was eight, and enrolled in Fourth Street School, finishing at the top of her class. The academic all-star continued through North Division High School and what is now the University of Wisconsin–Milwaukee. Decades later, as prime minister of Israel, Golda Meir would become one of the most celebrated citizens of the world.

By the time Golda left Milwaukee for Palestine in 1921, the formative years were nearly over for Milwaukee's Jewish community. Immigration slowed to a trickle, and the population evolved in place through the Depression, World War II, and a half-century of prosperity.

The 25,000 Jews in the Milwaukee area today reflect several generations of change in work, worship, and residential choice. As the community grew, its geographic orientation shifted from urban neighborhoods like Hillside and Sherman Park to the North Shore suburbs, including Fox Point, Bayside, and now Mequon. The varieties of religious expression have also broadened. Today's Jews range from the thoroughly secularized, to whom Judaism is largely a matter of surname and remembered foods, to the Orthodox, who observe no distinction between faith and life.

This increasingly diverse community has produced a number of notable leaders. Without Bud Selig, Milwaukee might not have major-league baseball. Without Ben Barkin, there might have been no Circus Parade. Without Ben and Steve Marcus, father and son, our choice of movie theaters and hotel rooms would be considerably narrower. And there is some irony in the fact that Wisconsin, not New York or Florida, has sent two Jews to the U.S. Senate at the same time: Herb Kohl and Russ Feingold.

More than 150 years after its founding, the Jewish community is well-established in Milwaukee, but some of its members are still putting down roots. At least 2,500 Russian Jews have settled here since 1990, and Shorewood has become their particular stronghold. What these newest of newcomers have found is precisely what every generation before them found: opportunity.

Despite the traumas of adjustment and periodic outbreaks of prejudice, Jews have had ample room to grow in Milwaukee. Golda Meir put it simply in a 1969 visit to her second hometown: "Before Milwaukee, I knew only the sorrows of the Jewish people in eastern Europe. Here in Milwaukee, I found freedom, kindness, and cleanliness."

Not the Promised Land, perhaps, but close enough.

School Children, 1890

Outrage Revisited
Bennett Law Furor of 1890 Set a Precedent

The political wildfire raged for months. In 2002, when Milwaukee County adopted an unusually generous pension plan, angry voters launched one of the most explosive protest movements in modern Wisconsin history. By the time it burned out, County Executive Tom Ament had resigned, several supervisors had been recalled, and a Republican, Scott Walker, held the highest office in what had once been a safely Democratic county.

Some reporters described the uproar as "history-making," but there were, as usual, ample precedents. More than once, Wisconsin voters have risen up in unison when they felt their interests being threatened. Economic interests were at the center of the 2002 pension scandal. In 1890, state residents sensed that something much broader was at stake: their way of life.

Milwaukee was the most "foreign" city in America at the time. In 1890, immigrants and their children made up an astounding 86.4 percent of the community's population. Many Milwaukee neighborhoods —German, Polish, Irish, and others—resembled urban villages, each built around a particular church and school. Fully aware of the erosive power of American culture, the newcomers hoped to raise their children, for as long as possible, in close contact with their ancestral language and religion. Parochial schools were bulwarks of ethnic identity.

The same pattern held true throughout Wisconsin, a situation that some political leaders—notably Yankee Republican leaders—found disquieting. Many feared that immigrants were holding their children too far outside the American mainstream. Gov. William Dempster Hoard, a Fort Atkinson newspaperman best-known as the dairy farmer's best friend, made the education issue uniquely his own. It was during his gubernatorial term that Wisconsin enacted the infamous Bennett Law.

The 1889 measure required Wisconsin children between the ages of seven and fourteen to attend school for at least twelve weeks each year—a provision that seems lax by modern standards. But the Bennett Law also required the teaching of "reading, writing, arithmetic and United States history, in the English language."

Those last four words dropped like matches into a pool of gasoline. Although the Bennett Law had passed with little debate, tempers flared as soon as its implications began to sink in. German Lutherans were the first to take offense. Pastors and synod leaders blasted the law as a frontal assault on their culture, their traditions, and their fundamental rights as American citizens. German and Polish Catholics (who seldom agreed with Lutherans on anything) soon picked up the chorus. They acknowledged the practical value of knowing English, but most were offended by the very idea of their children learning in what was, for most of them, still a foreign language.

Fed by incendiary sermons from a thousand pulpits, a firestorm of protest swept the state. No amount of explaining or temporizing from the law's supporters would do; voters wanted heads to roll. They did not yet have the power to recall public officials, but an election was not far off.

Oblivious to political realities, Gov. Hoard refused to back down, and Democrats, who had been locked out of power on the state and local levels for several years, sensed an opportunity. The Milwaukee branch of the party made a political neophyte, George W. Peck, their 1890 mayoral candidate. Peck's chief virtues were his opposition to the Bennett Law and his name recognition. Like Hoard, he was a newspaperman with roots in upstate New York, but George Peck had earned a national reputation as a humorist. *Peck's Bad Boy*, featuring a rascal named Hennery and the tricks he played on his bumbling Pa, became an American standard in the late 1800s. The stories hold up relatively well more than a century later; it's not hard to imagine Hennery and his Pa as prototypes for Bart and Homer Simpson.

The Bennett Law was George Peck's only campaign issue. He left the blistering rhetoric to others, stating mildly that parents should have the right to "bring up children in religion without being molested." When the votes were counted in April of 1890, Peck had won in a landslide, and anti-Bennett Germans took a majority of seats on the Common Council.

The new mayor barely had time to find the men's room in City Hall. Sensing momentum on their side, state Democrats nominated George Peck for governor in the November elections. Blasting Republicans for their "policy of paternalism" and "interference with parental rights," he won handily. Democrats captured both houses of the legislature and all but one congressional seat that fall, and William Dempster Hoard went home to Fort Atkinson.

The Bennett Law was quickly repealed in favor of a more generic school-attendance statute. Gov. Peck led the state for the next four years, earning a reputation as a fiscal conservative and, in historian Robert Nesbit's choice phrase, "one of the few intentional humorists among Wisconsin's governors."

Life in the state slowly returned to normal. The children of the immigrants learned English anyway, though on a more leisurely schedule, and George Peck ultimately returned to telling stories about the Bad Boy he had created in his pre-statehouse days. It was clear, however, that the Bennett Law had caused a more lasting change in the state's political landscape. By rallying immigrants together against a common enemy, it reinforced the very patterns of ethnic identity that the law's supporters had hoped to weaken.

Wisconsin's electorate has risen up several times since the Bennett Law furor. Voters have shown a remarkable ability to move from apathy to anger at the speed of sound, and generations of elected officials, on issues ranging from pensions to public education, have struggled to learn the same lesson: There are some things you tamper with only at the risk of your political skin.

Gesu Parish Church

Freeway to Oblivion

Marquette Interchange Erased
the Tory Hill Neighborhood

The Marquette Interchange is the busiest crossroads in Wisconsin. Joining two of the state's main-traveled roads in the heart of Milwaukee, it is the knot in the pretzel, the hub of the wheel, the point where all paths converge. But the interchange might be considered something else: Wisconsin's biggest gravestone. This monumental pile of concrete lies squarely on the site of a vanished neighborhood called Tory Hill.

Between 1870 and 1900, the blocks beneath the present Marquette Interchange sprouted a dense cluster of modest frame dwellings. They housed at least 300 families, many of them large, most of them Irish. Tory Hill, a name whose origin remains a mystery, was settled by people carried west on the swelling tide of Milwaukee's Irish migration. From their foothold in the Third Ward, Celtic families pushed across the Milwaukee River, creating Tory Hill in the 1870s and Merrill Park—west of Twenty-seventh Street—in the 1880s and '90s. One short street on the site of the interchange was named Hibernia—the Latin word for Ireland.

The attractions were obvious: cheap housing, plenty of jobs in the nearby Menomonee Valley, and strong community institutions. The most important anchor was Gesu Church. Generally considered Marquette University's campus church today, Gesu began as the center of Tory Hill's parish life. Dedicated in 1894, it provided a place of worship for thousands of Irish Catholics, and the parish school provided an education for nearly all their children.

One of Gesu's altar boys was a youngster named Pat O'Brien. Born in the O'Donnell Flats on Thirteenth and Clybourn Streets, O'Brien spent his formative years in Milwaukee and then moved on to stardom in Hollywood. He played the lead in dozens of films, including the 1940 hit *Knute Rockne, All-American*. Another Irishman of more local reputation was raised in the O'Donnell Flats: William O'Donnell, Milwaukee's county executive from 1976 to 1988. The O'Donnells, in fact, were the O'Brien family's landlords.

There were plenty of diversions for the young people of Tory Hill: sandlot baseball, programs at Gesu School, and unsupervised excursions into the Menomonee Valley. During the winter months, some of the more adventurous boys improvised a bobsled run that stretched from Wisconsin (then Grand) Avenue all the way to the valley floor—a distance of four hair-raising blocks.

Although it was a cohesive neighborhood, Tory Hill was anything but isolated. Grand Avenue, its northern border, was one of the finest residential streets in the city. James Kneeland, a well-heeled merchant, owned the entire block between Tenth and Eleventh Streets south of Grand. His estate included a small pond complete with a family of swans. Directly across the street stood First Methodist Church, a graceful Gothic structure with a pair of matching bell towers.

The landscape just south of Tory Hill was decidedly less picturesque. St. Paul Avenue, Clybourn Street, and the valley itself were lined with machine shops, planing mills, trunk factories, and dozens of other industries. The largest plant on St. Paul belonged to the National Enameling and Stamping Company, a tinware manufacturer better known by its initials: NESCO.

NESCO roasters poured out of Tory Hill well into the twentieth century, but the neighborhood never stood still. Marquette University, which started on the modest hilltop at Tenth and State Streets, moved to Grand Avenue in 1907, transforming the western perimeter of Tory Hill and creating a new mission for Gesu Church. The Kneeland mansion on Grand Avenue came down in the 1920s to make way for a courthouse that was ultimately built two blocks farther north. The old estate became Red Arrow Park, which featured a well-used wading pool on the site of the old swan pond.

As the Irish continued their slow migration westward, new ethnic groups moved into Tory Hill, including Croatians, Hungarians, and other southern and eastern Europeans. Hibernia Street still had a handful of McCarthys and Halligans in 1923, but the Rupena, Zivko, Vrotsovich, Petryczka, Miksa, and Kovarcevich families outnumbered them.

Industry, too, continued to evolve in place. Cutler-Hammer, a presence on St. Paul Avenue since 1899, grew rapidly in the first half of the twentieth century. As the market for its electrical controls soared, the firm bought out most of its neighbors, including the NESCO plant. By 1948, Cutler-Hammer occupied forty buildings spread across five city blocks on the southern edge of Tory Hill.

Shifting demographics and changing land use patterns created a different Tory Hill, but they were nothing compared to the cataclysm of the early 1960s. As planning for Milwaukee's freeway system gained momentum, county officials decided to replace the neighborhood with the Central Interchange, which they soon renamed for the adjacent university. The condemnation proceedings played no favorites. Red Arrow Park was demolished, First Methodist Church came tumbling down, and Cutler-Hammer, after extensive litigation, was forced to relocate. But it was the residential core of the neighborhood that suffered most. Work on the Marquette Interchange began in 1964. By the time it opened four years later, Tory Hill had been vaporized.

One new street in the freeway's shadow still carried the old name, and it survived the major reconstruction of the early 2000s. When the interchange first opened in 1968, "Tory Hill" reminded most passing motorists of what lay buried beneath, but the name's meaning has faded with the years. Today, as they navigate Wisconsin's major crossroads at speeds that would have stunned the early Irish, I wonder how many drivers realize that they're passing through the silent heart of a human community that once throbbed with life.

Miguel and Ana (Wrobel) Sevilla Chávez family in Mexico, 1949

Where Poland Meets Mexico
Milwaukee's South Side Blends Two Cultures

Arnoldo Sevilla and I have something in common. It's not just that we've known each other for thirty years, or that we share a passion for local history. The most interesting tie that binds us is our ethnic heritage. Although Arnoldo was born in Mexico and I was born in Milwaukee, we're both half Polish. My paternal ancestors emigrated from northwestern Poland in 1889, when my grandfather, another John Gurda, was still a boy. Arnoldo's maternal grandparents—John and Aniela Wrobel—came from the Warsaw area at the turn of the last century. Both of our families found work in Milwaukee, and they settled within a few blocks of each other on the city's South Side.

The similarities end there. My mother was a Norwegian immigrant's daughter who was raised on a dairy farm outside Coon Valley, Wisconsin. Arnoldo's father, Miguel Sevilla, was a native of west-central Mexico who came to Milwaukee in 1926 in search of work. The young man found a job at the Harnischfeger plant, and he found a lifelong partner on the South Side. When a mutual friend introduced him to Ana Wrobel, John and Aniela's daughter, a courtship developed. Accompanied by two guitar-playing friends, Miguel serenaded Ana with Spanish love songs from the sidewalk in front of her home—surely an unusual sight on S. Fifth Street. Her father was less than amused, but Ana was captivated. She and Miguel were married in 1931.

One year later, with the economy sinking into the trough of the Depression, Miguel took Ana home to his native state of Michoacan. There they remained for the rest of their lives, raising a family of twelve Mexican-Polish children. Arnoldo, the fifth-oldest, grew up in Mexico but moved to his mother's hometown in 1969. He has since become the leading historian of Milwaukee's Latino community and a highly respected local activist.

Arnoldo Sevilla embodies a connection between Poland and Latin America that is worth exploring. The two cultures are much closer than they might appear, and they are meeting with increasing frequency on

Milwaukee's South Side. The most compelling signs of ethnic change in my old neighborhood are political. In 1998, Pedro Colon, a lawyer born in Puerto Rico and raised in Milwaukee, won a seat in the Wisconsin Assembly. He took the spot vacated by Wally Kunicki, a proud son of the Polish South Side. In 2000, Jim Witkowiak, whose family's funeral home has been a Mitchell Street mainstay for decades, lost his aldermanic post to political newcomer Angel Sanchez, the son of Mexican immigrants. The symbolism of the shifts was obvious: In less than two years, a Kunicki gave way to a Colon and a Witkowiak to a Sanchez. Witkowiak later regained his seat, but in 2004, Peggy West (born Gonzalez) became the first Hispanic elected to the Milwaukee County Board.

Other signs of ethnic change may have escaped general notice. St. Stanislaus Catholic Church, whose twin gold spires are still a prominent Milwaukee landmark, was founded in 1866 as the first Polish church in urban America. St. Stan's now offers a Spanish-language Mass on Sunday, as do St. Hyacinth's, St. Adalbert's, and other historically Polish parishes. South Side priests report a common practice: They bury in Polish and baptize in Spanish.

Local businesses reflect the same shift. Twenty-five years ago, virtually all of Milwaukee's Mexican restaurants were located in Walker's Point, the area east of Sixteenth Street and north of Greenfield Avenue. Now Sixteenth Street has been renamed Cesar Chavez Drive, and Mexican restaurants can be found practically anywhere on the South Side. Lincoln Avenue—an old Polish shopping corridor—has one of my favorites: El Rey Sol. The restaurant is located just a few blocks from the site of my grandparents' old hardware store.

And then there are the taverns. The South Side has always had an impressive concentration of bars, most of them serving as communal living rooms for residents of the surrounding blocks. Those blocks are thoroughly mixed today, but the neighborhood's watering holes have become distinct cultural oases. It's not unusual for one bar to feature Frankie Yankovic on the jukebox and its neighbor to play nothing but Spanish songs. Year by year, however, the balance is shifting rapidly from polkas to *corridos* and *rancheras*.

All neighborhoods are changing neighborhoods, and Milwaukee's South Side is moving inexorably from a largely Polish residential base to a primarily Hispanic population. The transition is taking place without serious incident, perhaps because the major groups—Poles and Mexicans—have so much in common. The similarities are striking. Both groups are predominantly Catholic, both have a tradition of large and close-knit families, and both spoke a language other than English when they arrived. One group venerates Our Lady of Guadalupe, while the other prays to Our Lady of Czestochowa. Poles and Mexicans also began at the bottom of the economic ladder. They have struggled to overcome poverty as well as prejudice and, although their jobs were often dirty and dangerous, both groups earned reputations as untiringly hard workers.

The cultures are different, obviously, and there is no shortage of problems on the South Side, but I have long believed that Milwaukee's Mexican community is evolving along the same lines that characterized the city's Poles a generation or two earlier. On Milwaukee's South Side—whether your heritage is Polish, Mexican or, in Arnoldo Sevilla's case, both—the values of hard work and heritage translate easily.

Parade celebrating the return of the 32nd Division, 1919

Terrorism, Past Tense
When Patriotism Gives Way to Prejudice

The Abduls and Omars of America felt the heat. When terrorists attacked the United States on September 11, 2001, every Muhammad, Abu, and especially Osama in the country faced intense scrutiny from neighbors, co-workers and, in some cases, his own government. George W. Bush identified himself as a war president, and the resulting campaign against terrorism had some unforeseen, and unfortunate, cultural consequences. Arabs of many faiths and Muslims of many backgrounds reported that life after 9/11 was like walking on eggs.

A dwindling handful of Milwaukeeans might have found the pain of their Arab neighbors familiar. Some residents born early in the last century could have recalled a time when the Adolfs and Ottos of the community—the Dietrichs and Wolfgangs and Karls—suffered the same guilt by association as modern Muhammads. During the later stages of World War I, anyone suspected of harboring German blood became the target of unreasoning suspicion.

America was officially neutral when the shooting started in 1914. As residents of the most German city in the nation, Milwaukeeans felt free to express their support for the Kaiser's cause. In March 1916, local Germans and Austrians rented the Auditorium for a week-long "charity war bazaar" whose goal was the relief of "war sufferers" in the homeland. The event's organizers were not some splinter group of Teutonic militarists; they included Blatzes, Brumders, Vogels, Kletzsches, and other leading citizens. Nor was their bazaar a minor attraction; it drew 175,000 people—nearly half the city's population.

A dizzying about-face occurred as soon as America entered the war in 1917. As if to overcompensate for its earlier shows of sympathy, Milwaukee became a stronghold of anti-German feeling that quickly devolved into simple hysteria. Self-appointed patriots went looking for traitors and professed to find them everywhere—in classrooms, on the stage, even in the pulpit.

The super-patriots' ultimate goal was to rid the community of every last vestige of Germanism. In Milwaukee, that was a challenge equivalent to erasing a leopard's spots, but it didn't prevent a full-scale assault on Teutonic culture. German language instruction vanished from the public schools. Bach, Beethoven, and Brahms were banished from the concert stage. Literary giants like Goethe and Schiller disappeared from the classroom. Residents who failed to buy their full quota of Liberty Bonds found their houses splashed with yellow paint. As the pressures mounted, the German-English Academy was renamed Milwaukee University School, and the Deutscher Club became the Wisconsin Club. Even sauerkraut, that humblest of ethnic dishes, was reincarnated as "liberty cabbage."

The *Milwaukee Journal* gave voice to the sentiments of the super-patriots. F. Perry Olds, who had joined the paper just a year before, began to work a full-time disloyalty beat in 1916. Olds spent his days translating stories from Milwaukee's German-language press and publishing excerpts that he considered especially treasonous. The excerpts would fall easily under First Amendment rights today, but Olds' exposés were enough to win the *Journal* a Pulitzer Prize in 1919.

The campaign to stifle pro-German sentiment went far beyond words. By presidential decree, every "enemy alien" was required to register with federal authorities and obtain a special permit to live anywhere near a defense plant, which meant virtually everywhere in Milwaukee. The regulations complicated life for thousands of residents. The anti-German juggernaut kept rolling even after the Allies had won the war. In October 1919, nearly a year after the armistice was signed, the Pabst Theater tried to stage *Wilhelm Tell* in the original German. A hardy band of war veterans placed a cannon outside and promised some genuine fireworks if anyone so much as tried to raise the curtain.

The result of all the repression was a cultural rout. Milwaukee had once been known as the German Athens of America, a stronghold of drama, music, and fine art that anyone from the Fatherland could appreciate and enjoy. In the aftermath of World War I, that image vanished utterly. German ethnic identity, already fading in the bright light of New World prosperity, either disappeared or went into hiding, and with it went German culture.

It was not only the Germans who found themselves under attack. Milwaukee's Italians also felt the sting of public prejudice, largely as the result of a single, spectacular act of wartime terrorism. The incident began innocently enough. On September 9, 1917, a group of Methodists tried to stage a Sunday revival in the heart of Bay View's "Little Italy," at the intersection of Wentworth and Potter Avenues. The leader of the gathering was Rev. Augusto Giuliani, a former Catholic priest who had become a Protestant crusader. Giuliani ran a Methodist mission in the Third Ward, Milwaukee's largest Italian community, but he had designs on Bay View as well. Although an earlier visit had sparked violent protests, the firebrand returned on September 9, this time with police protection.

When Giuliani began to lead his followers in the singing of *America*, a scuffle broke out between protesters and police. An instant later, according to one eyewitness, "the shooting became general." When the gunfire was over, two protesters, both young Italian males, lay mortally wounded in the street, and two detectives were injured. The *Milwaukee Journal*, already famous for its high-pressure patriotism, pronounced the affair an "Anarchistic riot." The demonstrators, reported the paper, were not Catholics protecting their turf—the more logical explanation —but rather members of the Dramatic Lovers Social Study Club, a group the *Journal* characterized as anarchistic, anti-war, and anti-American.

Many of the group's members were arrested, but worse was yet to come. On November 24, as the Bay View Italians awaited trial, a suspicious package turned up outside Rev. Giuliani's church in the Third Ward. The pastor's assistant persuaded a neighbor to take the bundle to the central police station at Broadway and Wells Street. There, as officers were handling the package, it exploded with a blast that could be heard miles away. The front of the station house was practically blown off, and ten people were killed: nine police officers and a woman who had come downtown to file a complaint.

One of the first reporters on the scene described the explosion's grisly aftermath in terms reminiscent of 9/11: "Glass, plastering, clothing, arms, legs, papers, covered the floor. A cap from an officer's head hung on a broken bit of glass in a side window. . . . Strong men broke down as they cleared away the wreckage. . . . Those assisting in the removal of the victims picked up parts of bodies or scraped them into sheets with shovels."

The public, of course, was horrified. An intramural dispute between local Italians was one thing, but the senseless slaughter of Milwaukee's finest was the height of outrage. Mayor Daniel Hoan called the incident "a soul-sickening disaster." The Common Council blamed it on "the black hand of anarchy" and offered a $5,000 reward for information. Rumors swirled, every unmarked package seemed to conceal a bomb, and the entire city was on edge.

Milwaukee's Italians soon found themselves under siege. The police were ordered to "pick up and bring in any Italian who fails to give a good account of himself," and news stories were larded with casual stereotypes about violence and crime in the Italian community. ("Bombs the Particular Weapons of Sicilians," the *Milwaukee Journal* informed its readers.) The Italian consul felt compelled to describe his countrymen as "unfortunate in their quick tempers," The cumulative effect of the attention was a misplaced sense of collective guilt. "Just now," admitted one Third Ward resident, "I almost feel ashamed to step onto the street."

Most of the Italians arrested in the September riot were ultimately deported, but the makers of the "infernal machine" that killed nine policemen were never found. What prompted the bomb? Rev. Giuliani had a ready answer: "The Bay View Italians hate me and my church because in addition to the regular services we often had meetings at which we advocated patriotism and true Americanism."

Bay View had its share of radicals, but you'd think that opponents of the war effort would have blown up a defense plant before they tried to bomb a tiny Protestant mission. John Travis, a Bay View barber, offered another explanation. "We are not anarchists," said Travis, "but loyal American citizens and a peaceable community. We object however to having religion crammed down our throats." The barber traced the entire tragedy to Giuliani's insistence on "speaking to those who did not want to hear him."

For both the Germans and the Italians, tensions subsided with the passage of time—as they undoubtedly will for the Arab community. But the waves of suspicion did not pass without sapping the cultural vitality of two major Milwaukee ethnic groups. Many years later, there is still a lesson to be learned from the clashes of the World War I era. Intolerance thrives during times of insecurity. More than once, our ancestors confused enemies abroad with neighbors at home. When the next threat to our security emerges, may we have the wisdom and strength to avoid making the same mistake.

Water
The City's Lifeblood

Milwaukee River, ca. 1870

MILWAUKEE RIVER, AT MILWAUKEE.

Milwaukee River, 1874

Roots in the River

Milwaukee Rediscovers Its Other *Shoreline*

The Milwaukee River is alive again. Once given up for dead, the stream that defines and divides Milwaukee's downtown now pulses with new energy. A stunning Riverwalk runs the length of the business district. Riverside restaurants and nightclubs have multiplied. A steady stream of boats, from kayaks to cabin cruisers, ply the waters every summer weekend, and festivals, concerts, and races draw thousands of visitors.

The Milwaukee River's return is undoubtedly welcome and certainly overdue, but the stream should be viewed as much more than a neglected resource. In the long view, it is nothing less than the reason for Milwaukee's existence.

Understanding the river's historic role requires a little imagination. In the 1830s, when white settlement in the region began, nearly everyone who came west came by water. The Erie Canal carried travelers across New York State from Albany to Buffalo, where they boarded ships for destinations on Lakes Erie, Huron, and finally Michigan. The future clearly belonged to sites with superior harbors, and harbors, in those days, meant rivers. From Algoma and Manitowoc to Racine and Chicago, settlements sprouted wherever a river met the lake.

Milwaukee, it so happened, had both the deepest bay and the largest river on the western shore of Lake Michigan. Fed by the Menomonee, the Milwaukee River reached a depth of eighteen feet near its mouth—more than enough for the largest ships on the lakes. Speculators flocked to a location with such stellar potential. Byron Kilbourn, the West Side's founder, called Milwaukee "the most beautiful natural site for a large city, which has fallen under my observation."

For all its virtues, the would-be metropolis had a few flaws. Most of its present downtown was a swamp, and a sandbar at the river mouth blocked access to all but the smallest vessels. Those problems were solved in due course, and Milwaukee took its place among the busiest ports on the Great Lakes. The inner harbor was its only harbor at the time. Schooners and steamships ascended the river as far north as Humboldt Avenue, calling on the grain elevators, lumberyards, tanneries, and factories that lined both banks. From April to November, the downtown riverfront was literally a thicket of masts.

Conflict between lake and land traffic was inevitable and constant. In June 1855, for instance, the *Milwaukee Sentinel* reported that one schooner had kept the Water Street bridge open for more than an hour, "delaying the mail . . . , innumerable pedestrians, sixty-five teams [of horses] north, and forty-seven south of the bridge." Frequent bridge openings remained a headache for nearly a century.

Decades of heavy use and unrelenting urban growth created other problems for the river. By the late 1800s, it was playing an unwelcome role as Milwaukee's principal gutter, a channel for carrying off the waste of a city whose population was more than doubling every fifteen years. The results were predictable. When a *Harper's Monthly* reporter described the river in 1881, you could practically see him holding his nose: "It is a . . . currentless and yellowish murky stream, with water like oil, and an odor combined of the effluvia of a hundred sewers."

In 1888, Milwaukee "solved" its river problem by opening a tunnel between Lake Michigan (near the Milwaukee Yacht Club) and the North Avenue dam. Fresh lake water was pumped into the river, flushing the noxious wastes out of sight, out of mind—and out into the lake, where they aggravated an already staggering pollution problem. It was not until 1925, when the Jones Island sewage treatment plant opened, that water quality began to improve. Four years later, the Island's first port facilities were finished, relieving pressure on the Milwaukee River.

The city had turned its back on the stream by that time. Years before Jones Island was transformed, a local engineering society seriously proposed covering the river to create "a great boulevard" through the heart of downtown. There was an abundance of other plans and proposals in the decades that followed, but none could disguise the fact that the river had become a hardened artery of commerce. By the 1960s, it was nearly as dead as the alewives that drifted in its slack current.

It has only been since the 1980s, particularly during Mayor John Norquist's tenure (1988–2004), that Milwaukee began to rediscover its second shoreline. Norquist was a vocal champion of the Riverwalk District, and the Riverwalk, in turn, helped spawn new businesses, nightspots, and housing developments. The attention was appropriate. The downtown stream was like an old companion who had dropped out of the city's life for a few decades and was suddenly back in circulation. As its rebirth continues, Milwaukee is finally coming home to its roots in the river.

Milwaukee car ferry, built 1903

"Lake Michigan Bridged"

Lake Express Is the Latest Attempt to Bypass Chicago

The "Chicago penalty," my family calls it. Like everyone else in Wisconsin, we've come to expect heavy traffic, rude drivers, and constant construction as soon as we cross the Illinois border. If we're headed for points farther east, we time our trip to miss the worst of the gridlock, but there's no escaping at least an hour of white-knuckle driving before the tension starts to lift somewhere east of Gary.

With the 2004 debut of the *Lake Express*, a high-tech, high-speed ferry, Wisconsinites had a new way to avoid paying the Chicago penalty. The ferry put Muskegon within two-and-a-half hours of Milwaukee—faster than an Indy 500 driver could make the trip by land. The new craft was at the cutting edge of marine technology, but it rekindled an ancient Milwaukee dream: bypassing Chicago. That dream, in fact, has been a local preoccupation from the very beginning, and there was once considerably more at stake than a couple hours of driving time.

In the 1830s, when the city was founded, virtually everyone arrived by water, taking an Erie Canal boat across New York State and then boarding a ship at Buffalo for the trip west to Lake Michigan. The pioneers had every reason to expect great things. Ninety miles closer to the East than Chicago, and blessed with a better harbor, their little frontier settlement seemed destined to become "the Queen City of the Lakes." For more than a decade, Milwaukee and Chicago were in a virtual dead heat as population centers.

Then came the railroads. In the 1850s, completion of rail links to the east and west pushed Chicago to the front ranks of America's cities. Nestled at the foot of Lake Michigan, it became a natural hub for every rail line that crossed the northern United States. From 30,000 residents in 1850, Chicago's population swelled to 112,000 in 1860. Milwaukee's own population more than doubled during the same decade, passing the 45,000 mark in 1860, but that was scant comfort. Once closer to the

Atlantic seaboard than Chicago, the city was now ninety miles farther away by the main-traveled route. Wisconsin's metropolis began to feel the growing shade of a giant to its south.

Although the geographic realities were obvious, Milwaukee was not about to throw in the towel. The most practical alternative was to bypass Chicago by water. Milwaukee was already building railroads to the Mississippi in the 1850s, and the city had high hopes for a companion line taking shape on the Michigan side of the lake. That line, the Detroit & Milwaukee, was pushing steadily west to Grand Haven, directly opposite Milwaukee. The idea was to coordinate rail schedules in both directions with cross-lake "ferry steamers," providing a convenient hybrid route from the Atlantic to the Mississippi.

In 1853, Mayor George Walker, taking direct aim at Chicago, predicted that the Milwaukee-Grand Haven link would become "the great thoroughfare for trade, travel and emigration between the East and the West." The publisher of the 1857 city directory was even more hopeful: "The opening of this grand chain of Railways, all the way from the St. Lawrence and the Atlantic sea ports, to Grand Haven, on Lake Michigan, will bring Milwaukee directly into line, and make her the most important and the heaviest receiving and distributing point, for freight, produce, and passengers, in the entire North West." The Grand Haven connection was completed in 1858, and it did attract plenty of customers. The line's appeal was summed up in a clever newspaper ad: "Lake Michigan Bridged."

For all its virtues, the bridge failed to restore Milwaukee to parity with Chicago. Freight-handlers, in particular, disliked the "break bulk" nature of the service. Cargoes had to be unloaded from trains on one side of the lake and then reloaded on the other—hardly a model of efficiency.

Chicago, in the meantime, had become America's "Second City," but growth had its price. In the late 1800s, the city's railyards were every bit as congested as its freeways are today. Shippers continued to seek alternatives to travel around the lake, and service across the lake, on ships large enough to carry whole trains, was the next step. In 1892, the first rail ferry on Lake Michigan went into service between Frankfort, Michigan, and Kewaunee, Wisconsin. Within a decade or two, the lake was criss-crossed with lines that touched more than a dozen ports.

In 1897, service began between Milwaukee and Muskegon, a harbor town that had eclipsed nearby Grand Haven. Other lines followed in the 1900s, including the Pere Marquette (later Chesapeake & Ohio) and the Grand Trunk, both of which built docks that are still part of Milwaukee's waterfront. Local industries sent tons of freight across the lake every day for decades, but the car ferry companies discovered a new cargo in the 1920s: automobiles. Detroit's newest models came west for sale, and Milwaukee's lakefront came to resemble a gigantic parking lot at the peak of each model year.

There was a steady stream of travelers in the opposite direction. As tourists flocked to the ferries, ships built for freightcars took on family sedans as well. The tourist trade showed such promise, in fact, that a pair of Muskegon promoters decided to capitalize on it. In 1941, they launched the *Milwaukee Clipper*, a rebuilt 1904 steamer featuring air-conditioned staterooms, a movie theater, and a dance floor. For tens of thousands of Wisconsinites, taking the *Clipper* to Muskegon was the closest they ever came to a genuine cruise experience.

The railroad ferries tried to reach the same trade. In 1953, the Chesapeake & Ohio commissioned two behemoths that carried both rail and passenger cars. Christened the *Badger* and the *Spartan*, after college teams on both sides of the lake, the ferries were promoted as the "twin queens" of the C&O fleet.

All too soon, it was over. The *Milwaukee Clipper* made its last regular run in 1970, and the C&O discontinued ferry service from Milwaukee in 1980. Trucks, freeways, and economics had caught up with both of them. The updated *Badger* ultimately found a new home on the Manitowoc-Ludington run, but Milwaukee was without a car ferry for nearly a quarter-century.

The Chicago penalty, meanwhile, was getting stiffer every year, and in 2004, a group of risk-tolerant local investors decided to give travelers an open-water alternative. The *Lake Express* is only a ship, I know, but it's also a sleek expression of an ancient Milwaukee impulse. The ferry revived a cross-lake tradition that's more than 150 years old, and it recalled a faded dream of regional supremacy. Despite Milwaukee's best efforts, Chicago became the greater city. There's no getting around it, I suppose—unless you take the ferry.

Jones Island, 1916

At Home on Jones Island

Modern Port Once Harbored a Polish Fishing Village

In a city known for its public green spaces, Kaszube's Park is hardly a standout. One picnic table, a lone willow tree, and an old anchor are its only features, and all have seen better days. But the park, a narrow city lot on the western edge of Milwaukee's Jones Island, is the last trace of a fishing village that was once unique in urban America.

The Island—actually a peninsula—was named for Capt. James Monroe Jones, an Ohio farmer's son who turned to the Great Lakes for his livelihood. In 1854, Capt. Jones built a shipyard at the mouth of the Milwaukee River, on the present site of the city's sewage treatment plant. It prospered until 1858, when a violent storm literally washed the business away.

Ten or fifteen years later, fishing families began to colonize the wasteland near the river mouth. There were perhaps a dozen houses on Jones Island in 1875. By 1900, the number had swelled to 300, and the Island's population reached a peak of at least 1,500. Like mainland Milwaukee, the settlement was ethnically diverse. Jones Island had hundreds of German-speaking Pomeranians and a handful of Scandinavians, but both groups were outnumbered by Kaszubs (kah-*shoobs*), a people who had emigrated from the Baltic seacoast of Poland. Their former home, in fact, was another windswept spit of sand: the Hel Peninsula north of Gdansk.

The Kaszubs' dialect and customs set them apart from their fellow Poles, in both the Old World and the New. Their primary occupation was just as distinctive. As Polish immigrants on the South Side adjusted to jobs in Milwaukee's factories, the Kaszubs of Jones Island continued a way of life they had known for centuries: fishing. By 1900, their community was the center of commercial fishing in southeastern Wisconsin. First in sailboats and later in steam tugs, intrepid Islanders set out each morning in search of trout, whitefish, perch, herring, and sturgeon. Nearly 175 men hoisted nets for a living, and their catch totaled two million pounds in a good year. Most of it came to market through wholesalers, but a sizable crew of Islanders peddled fish, both fresh and smoked, from door to door on the mainland.

The settlement's landscape was just as unique as its economy. Jones Island's street "system" was a chaotic maze that even frequent visitors found disorienting, and its houses ranged from scrap-lumber shacks to sizable Victorian homes. Along the margins of this urban village were backyard boat docks, weather-beaten fish sheds, and scores of oversized net reels. Barely a mile from downtown, Jones Island offered some of the most picturesque scenery in the region, and it attracted scores of artists and art students, among them a young Carl Sandburg.

Another type of tourism was crucial to the local economy. There were at least eleven saloons on the Island at the turn of the century, and many offered fish fries and crab boils that drew crowds of visitors from the mainland. In 1903, Charles Plambeck, the Island's unofficial "governor," began a regular launch service from the Wisconsin Avenue bridge to the dock of his saloon and restaurant.

This colorful chapter in Milwaukee's history ended prematurely. Most of the Islanders occupied their land without benefit of title, and their position at the river mouth made them vulnerable. When the Illinois Steel Company, whose gigantic mill covered the southern end of the peninsula, wanted better docking facilities, its leaders looked north to Jones Island. In 1896, claiming prior title to the land, they sued to evict the Islanders, one by one. The Kaszubs and their neighbors resisted, claiming "adverse occupancy" or, in plain English, squatter's rights.

The City of Milwaukee, in the meantime, developed an urgent need for both an outer harbor and sewage treatment facilities. Local officials had long treated the Islanders with a blend of indifference and scorn. In 1911, the Sewerage Commission picked Jones Island as their plant site "because of its isolation and especially its remoteness from residential districts." The Island's potential for harbor development was even more obvious. In 1914, while the Illinois Steel cases were still dragging through the courts, the City of Milwaukee began condemnation proceedings.

Squeezed between local government on one side and Illinois Steel on the other, the Islanders had little choice but to hoist their anchors.

By 1920, only twenty-five families remained, and their numbers dwindled steadily. A handful of holdouts lingered on the western edge of the settlement, around the present site of Kaszube's Park. Their leader was Capt. Felix Struck, a tavern-keeper who happened to be the first child born on the Island. He was also the last to leave. Struck stood his ground until 1943, when authorities removed the seventy-four-year-old Kaszub for reasons of "port security." Less than six months later, Capt. Struck was dead.

Jones Island today is an urban wilderness, a place where no one lives and few people visit. My family and I are among the visitors, biking down from our home in Bay View on occasional summer evenings. We pedal through a landscape that has become pure geometry, passing under the graceful arch of the Hoan Bridge and past the squat cylinders of petroleum tanks, the oblong freight containers stacked on the docks, and massive mounds of tarp-covered road salt. Our journey always ends at Kaszube's Park—the only intentional green space in that abstract landscape, and the last reminder that Jones Island was once a living, breathing human community.

Milwaukee Flushing Station

The Flush of Success

Alterra Coffee and Sewerage
District Brew an Unlikely Winner

There's nothing quite like it anywhere in Wisconsin. Where else can you find an upscale coffeehouse sharing quarters with a technology museum in a pump house built to relieve a horrific water pollution problem? The combination may seem unlikely, but that's exactly what you'll see at 1701 N. Lincoln Memorial Drive, where Alterra Coffee Roasters and the Milwaukee Metropolitan Sewerage District jointly occupy the Milwaukee River Flushing Station.

In one half of the lakefront landmark, Alterra offers a full menu of food and beverages, including eggplant panini and blackened tuna salad served with honey latte or iced chai. In the other half, MMSD maintains educational displays that include a working model of its deep-tunnel system. Beneath them both lies a water pump that was once the largest in the world, with a propeller fourteen feet in diameter. Like the espresso machines upstairs, it still works.

The pump was installed to remedy a nineteenth-century problem delicately referred to as "the river nuisance." The lower Milwaukee River was a lively stream in its native state, but decades of dredging and docking had turned it into an estuary—an inlet of the lake whose current was barely perceptible. There were times, in fact, when the river actually flowed backward, a phenomenon that can still be observed occasionally today.

The becalmed river became a watery grave for all sorts of urban waste, including tons of horse manure that plopped onto the city's streets every day and washed into the stream with the next rain. By the 1870s, the city faced a pollution problem of epic proportions. Summer heat turned the slack, scum-covered waters of the river into a noxious stew whose smell was almost overpowering. Contemporary observers left no adjective unturned in describing the stream. "Filthy, villainous, unhealthy, plague-breeding," offered one reporter. Another wrote that the prevailing stench "made the average mortal wish he had been born without nostrils." The chorus continued: "sickening," "deplorable," "intolerable," "vile and offensive," "unendurable." "Simply disgusting," added a visiting lady lecturer. "Why, I nearly stifled as the steamer came up the harbor this morning."

Something obviously had to be done. No one suggested diapering the horses or closing the tanneries and breweries. The simplest "solution," some believed, was to open the North Avenue dam every so often and push the accumulated filth out into the lake. The city's engineers, however, concluded that opening the dam would simply mix the soup without removing it, and that it would take three weeks for the pool upstream to recharge. Others favored pumping Milwaukee's wastewater over the glacial divide west of town and into some river that would carry the problem to the Mississippi.

Milwaukee finally settled on a system of intercepting sewers. Lines running parallel to the main rivers would capture the liquid waste and convey it to a station on Jones Island, from which it would be pumped into Lake Michigan. The Menomonee Valley portion of the intercepting system was largely completed by 1887, but city officials chose an alternate course for the Milwaukee River. Why not, they wondered, dig a tunnel under the East Side and pump fresh lake water into the putrid river, giving it enough force to cleanse its lower reaches? Why not flush?

That was precisely what they did. Workers dug a horizontal hole, twelve feet in diameter and a half-mile long, between Lake Michigan and a river outlet just below the North Avenue dam. They also dredged a lake inlet, now lined with concrete walls, that is still a popular fishing spot. The inlet fed a huge, steam-driven pump designed by Milwaukee's own E.P. Allis Company, a forerunner of Allis-Chalmers. The pump's centerpiece was a *Titanic*-sized propeller capable of moving nearly 6,000 gallons of water every second. Both pump and propeller were enclosed in a handsome Romanesque building that might have been mistaken for a Turner hall or a school.

The "flushing works" was completed in September 1888, at a total cost of $240,774.88. Milwaukee thought its problems were over. The Allis pump could replace the entire contents of the river below the dam every twenty-four hours. "This immense volume of water keeps the river in very fine condition," wrote city engineer George Benzenberg, "and tends to cool the air along its shore during hot days."

Another problem surfaced soon enough. Lake Michigan's long-shore currents generally move from north to south in the Milwaukee area, but contrary weather sometimes pushed the plume of river sewage in the opposite direction—right over the city's water intakes at North Point. Milwaukeeans began to suffer regular epidemics of "intestinal flu," and it didn't take a trained hydrologist to identify the culprit. The city started adding chlorine to its drinking water in 1910, but it was not until 1925, when the Jones Island treatment plant opened, that the sewage threat was largely neutralized.

We have traveled light-years from the time when Milwaukee's main river was literally an open sewer. No one would confuse the downtown channel with a trout stream today, but its water quality is immeasurably better than it was in the 1880s. The Flushing Station, built as a monument to desperation, has become a working antique, its pump operated only occasionally for "general maintenance purposes."

Now the station serves a different purpose. The partnership between Alterra Coffee Roasters and the Sewerage District preserves one of Milwaukee's most distinctive landmarks. That, I think, is grounds for applause, but there's also an irresistible irony on the lakefront: A high-end coffeehouse is now selling beverages in a facility designed to move a far murkier liquid.

Summer

Summer 1901

Isabella Mitchell and William Mackie

Wedding of the Century
Mitchell-Mackie Nuptials of 1881 Raised the Bar

every wedding season brings the same sights and sounds. Crepe-papered cars cruise by with their horns blaring on Saturday mornings, couples pose for pictures in the fanciest clothes they will ever wear, and even the humblest halls are filled for receptions. Some events might tax the ingenuity of local caterers (and the pocketbooks of doting parents), but not many can rival a wedding that took place on August 3, 1881. That ceremony united a Scottish doctor, William Mackie, with a Scottish farmer's daughter, Isabella Mitchell, and it was widely considered the social event of the century.

Isabella happened to be a favorite niece of Alexander Mitchell, the wealthiest man in Wisconsin. Since his own arrival from Scotland in 1839, Mitchell had built an empire whose cornerstones were the Marine Bank, the Milwaukee Road, and Northwestern National Insurance. Mitchell's home was a conspicuous symbol of his success. The entrepreneur's estate covered nearly the entire square block between Ninth and Tenth Streets north of Wisconsin Avenue, and at its center was a sprawling mansion built in the French style. That mansion, substantially remodeled, is still very much in use as the Wisconsin Club.

Although he generally fit the stereotype of the tight-fisted Scot, Alexander Mitchell made an exception for his niece and nephew-to-be. The Mitchell-Mackie wedding and the reception that followed were both held in his mansion, and the master of the house kept a small army of decorators busy for weeks before the event.

The ceremony itself was simple enough: a formal exchange of vows before a handful of relatives, a few close friends, and an Episcopal priest. The setting was anything but simple. William and Isabella were married beneath a bower of palms in the just-completed Oriental Room, a Victorian fantasy with silk-upholstered furniture, walls of hand-painted felt, and a profusion of silk drapes.

The guests began to arrive immediately after the ceremony. Nearly 1,200 people flocked to the mansion, including Milwaukee's business and professional elite, Wisconsin's leading politicians, and a sprinkling of millionaires from Chicago and beyond. As they waited to congratulate the newlyweds, Mitchell's guests enjoyed one of the most elaborate floral displays the city had ever seen. "Magnificent bunches of variegated and odorous blossoms occupied every point of advantage within the ducal residence," reported the *Milwaukee Sentinel*, and the spectacle included hundreds of flowers from Mitchell's own greenhouses. One massive arrangement spelled out the couple's initials—"M and M"—in tube roses against a background of lilies, carnations, and heliotropes. Just to make sure his guests knew who was paying for all this splendor, Alexander Mitchell had his florists build another bank of blossoms with "AM" at the center.

The grounds of the estate were, if possible, even more lavishly appointed. Guests marveled at the carpeted walkways, illuminated fountains, and trees festooned with "innumerable" Chinese lanterns. At the heart of the grounds was a dancing pavilion that looked like something out of Camelot. The poles of this oversized tent were topped with eighty silk pennants, including the flags of Scotland, America, England, France, and Germany. Inside the pavilion were coats of arms representing the McKenzies, McGregors, MacDonalds, and a dozen more Scottish clans. Other decorations ranged from busts of Walter Scott and Robert Burns to a painting of Cupid perched inside a wedding ring. Local reporters could hardly find words to describe the scene. Mitchell's estate, gushed the *Sentinel*, had been transformed into "a purely mythological retreat" that "called up the recollection of stories from the Arabian nights." The *Evening Wisconsin* praised the "indescribably beautiful" decorations as "a triumph of art and genius."

Culinary genius was evident as well. The lucky guests dined on "everything tempting," reported the *Sentinel*, "in or out of season." The rarer delicacies included boned turkey with truffles, sweetbread salad, buffalo tongue with jelly, pickled oysters, and salmon salad with capers. Dinner was followed by seven kinds of ice cream, a variety of puddings and fruits, and, of course, wedding cake. The assembled blue-bloods put away nearly 200 pounds of bride's cake, groom's cake, chocolate cake, coconut cake, and white almond cake.

At the center of the throng were Dr. and Mrs. Mackie. The groom wore a traditional black suit with white gloves, but Isabella was decked out like a wedding cake herself. The bride's dress, according to one reporter, was of "heavy ivory satin, garnished elaborately with a pineapple pattern of Irish point lace . . . in deep flounces." The bridal outfit included a full train and a long tulle veil held in place by a coronet of pearls.

It was midnight before Isabella finally traded her heavy dress for a "handsome traveling costume." After hugs and handshakes all around, the newlyweds boarded a special train bound for Chicago and points east. Their honeymoon would last for six weeks.

The celebration presumably continued into the early morning hours. When the last Chinese lantern had been extinguished and the last bottle of fine wine had been emptied, it was clear that the event had set a new standard for local entertaining. The *Evening Wisconsin* called the Mitchell-Mackie wedding the "most brilliant event in Milwaukee social history," without the slightest fear of contradiction. Using the wealth he commanded as Wisconsin's king of capital, Alexander Mitchell threw a party fit for royalty, and the memory of its splendid excesses lingered for decades, even among the common folk who had only watched at the gate.

Iron workers of the Bay View Rolling Mill

Meltdown at the Iron Mill
Heat Was Harder to Bear in 1881

S ummer heat often comes as a shock in the North. After those first, delicious days when we can finally wear short sleeves again, we seem to proceed directly to weeks of melting blacktop and clothes that stick to our skins. Some residents—foundry workers, short-order cooks, roofers—feel the heat in all its searing intensity, but many of us spend the summer moving between air-conditioned homes and air-conditioned offices in air-conditioned cars. Only when we're outside do we Northerners get a glimpse of what Miami and Houston face all summer long.

Our ancestors weren't so lucky. They were helpless against the heat, and some workplaces were practically hell on earth. Milwaukee's most infernal employer may have been the Bay View iron mill. Established in 1866 as the Milwaukee Iron Company, the mill dominated the lakefront on what is now the southern end of the Dan Hoan Bridge. Its massive blast furnaces lit the nighttime sky over Bay View with a fiery red glow in every season. By the mid-1870s, the mill was the second-largest producer of railroad rails in America and Milwaukee's largest employer by a wide margin. Nearly 1,500 men reported for work in Bay View during peak periods, considerably more than the number punching in today at such manufacturing mainstays as Ladish and Falk.

It was not work for the weak of heart. In 1881, the *Milwaukee Sentinel* dispatched a reporter to visit the mill during a heat wave. What he found would have horrified any modern safety and health inspector. Puddlers, the skilled workers who tended the blast furnaces, routinely endured temperatures exceeding 160 degrees. They spent twelve hours a day, six days a week, producing caldrons of liquid iron, and workers down the line fared no better. Some rolled red-hot ingots fresh from the furnace into rails, and others stacked them while they were still glowing. The *Sentinel* reporter could hardly believe his eyes: "None but the men who have worked in these great hives of human industry, among immense furnaces and molten and seething metal, have any conception of the heat which a mill-hand has to endure while at his hard and tedious labor."

The workers had few defenses. There were no electric fans, because there was no electricity. The furnace crews generally worked bare-chested, with Turkish towels wrapped around their necks to soak up some of the sweat and leather straps over their hob-nailed boots to prevent burns from spilled iron. Every worker downed two to three buckets of "oatmeal water" during his shift, usually laced with lemon juice.

For this most hazardous of all hazardous duty, the skilled workers earned $5 a day. That was a princely sum in 1881, but it translates to only $7 an hour in modern terms, even after more than a century of inflation—and that's without a dime in fringe benefits. Unskilled workers, who often experienced the same heat, earned only $1.15 for their twelve-hour days.

Back in the safe haven of his office, the *Sentinel* correspondent could afford to wax philosophical. "No one is to blame for it all," he wrote. "Railways must be constructed. No one has been able to concoct a drink, which will drive away the deathly thirst of the men who make the rails, or to invent a fan that will keep the mills cool in summer. The men are satisfied with their pay and must be satisfied with the weather."

Bay View's mill workers were not nearly as passive as the reporter portrayed them. The skilled hands organized a union called the Sons of Vulcan soon after the plant opened, and in 1872 they dedicated Puddlers Hall as their headquarters. Now operating as a tavern at 2463 S. St. Clair Street, Puddlers Hall is certainly one of the oldest labor landmarks in the Midwest, if not the nation.

The Sons of Vulcan and its successors were among the strongest unions in Milwaukee, and labor disputes were a regular feature of the summer months in Bay View. Most concerned wage rates, but not all. In 1873, nine heaters walked off the job to protest excessive temperatures. They were promptly fired, a move that stirred the union to call a walkout of 900 employees. Production quickly ground to a halt.

"The position of a heater is not an envious one," said one of the discharged workers, in a triumph of understatement. "He is constantly looking into a furnace of molten iron, with hot iron and other furnaces around him. In cold weather the perspiration steams from them, and in hot weather with no breeze it is scarcely bearable." The men returned to work in a week, presumably after the heat had subsided to less hellish levels.

The Bay View iron mill remained in business until 1929. Its owner, United States Steel, had been steadily shifting jobs to its enormous complex in Gary, Indiana, where conditions were probably just as inhuman. After a lengthy tussle between the company and the City of Milwaukee, the site was cleared for redevelopment.

Today the old mill grounds are occupied by the Coast Guard Station, the Naval Reserve Center, and the Bay View end of the Hoan Bridge. Only the ghosts remain, along with fading memories of a storied period in both the neighborhood's history and the industrial history of Milwaukee. When the mercury rises in mid-summer, step out of your air-conditioned cocoon for a moment and raise a glass of oatmeal water to the mill hands of 1881. They were men of iron, concluded the *Sentinel* reporter, "who become red hot and yet do not melt."

Mayor Carl Zeidler

Milwaukee's Singing Mayors
Fourth of July Has Always Been a Test of Endurance

Most cities have mayors who sing. Municipal leaders are generally expected to lift their voices in melody, even if it's only to struggle through *The Star-Spangled Banner* at baseball games. Milwaukee has a different tradition: singing mayors. For more than fifty years, the city had a succession of top officials who made song part of their political signature, and the Fourth of July was their moment to shine.

In a town once filled with German choral groups, politicians with names like Wallber, Koch, Rauschenberger, and Seidel could generally hold their own when the band started playing, but the singing-mayor tradition really began with Carl Zeidler. In the late 1930s, Zeidler was a young assistant city attorney with vivid dreams of higher office. Long before he announced his run for mayor in 1940, Zeidler was appearing before any group that would host him.

Blonde, good-looking, and helplessly extroverted, he seemed to be everywhere, shaking hands, making speeches and, wherever he went, singing songs. Blessed with a fine baritone voice, Zeidler was already known for his work with Lutheran, Methodist, and Episcopal church choirs as well as the Liederkranz male chorus and a quartet called the Milwaukeeans. During his mayoral campaign, the candidate made hundreds of appearances as a solo performer. *God Bless America* was his standard number, but the young attorney could also belt out crowd-pleasers like *Battle Hymn of the Republic* and *The Road to Mandalay*.

Carl Zeidler won the 1940 election, ending the twenty-four-year tenure of Socialist Dan Hoan. "Here is a young man who actually sings for his votes," reported the *New York Times*, "and the people apparently love it." The *Times* called Zeidler's victory a demonstration of "music's power to soothe the elector's breast."

The new mayor continued to sing after taking office. On July 4, 1940, Zeidler attended every park celebration in the city, covering roughly 100 miles between 9 a.m. and 8:32 p.m. He entertained nearly 85,000 people with fifteen short speeches on democracy and a variety of songs, including *God Bless America* five times and *John Brown's Body* and *The Old Mill Stream* (with gestures) once each. By the time he crawled into bed that night, Zeidler had set a precedent that most of his successors have tried hard to follow.

Mayor Zeidler left City Hall to join the Naval Reserve soon after the bombing of Pearl Harbor. His golden baritone was stilled forever in 1942, when a German submarine sank his ship in the south Atlantic. John Bohn led a caretaker administration for six years after Zeidler's disappearance. Seventy-five years old when he took office, Bohn made no attempt to match his predecessor's pace or musical proficiency. Then, in 1948, Carl's younger brother, Frank Zeidler, won the city's top job. Although he once sang a duet with Hildegarde on the stage of the Auditorium, Milwaukee's last (or perhaps most recent) Socialist mayor disclaimed any musical ability. "Carl got his talent from our father's side," he said, "I have a hard time carrying a tune." But Frank Zeidler never stayed at home on the Fourth of July. During his twelve years in office, the mayor typically gave seventeen speeches every Independence Day, all of them extemporaneous. "It's not hard," Zeidler said with typical modesty, "You pick a theme and find the words to express it."

And then there was Henry Maier. As Milwaukee's mayor from 1960 to 1988—a record that may stand forever—Maier took himself with the utmost seriousness, and that trait extended to music. Determined to improve his self-described "lyric tenor," Maier studied diligently under a local voice teacher. Although he was perfectly adequate as a song leader, the mayor's training produced a voice that *Milwaukee Journal* reporter David Umhoefer aptly described as an "operatic growl."

Henry Maier kept up the blistering pace of his predecessors on the Fourth of July, bringing his growl to bear on patriotic standards, ethnic tunes, and even his own composition, *The Summerfest Polka*. Maier's lyrics merit some kind of musical immortality:

Go to Milwaukee!
How humming a city you'll see.
Sing in Milwaukee!
Trah, lah, lah, lah, lee.

Prosit, Milwaukee!
Toast gaily and so free.
Milwaukee, Milwaukee, Milwaukee!
A happy place to be.

John Norquist, who took office in 1988, continued the Zeidler/ Maier Fourth of July tradition, but he broadened the mayoral repertoire considerably. On the South Side, Norquist might have wrapped his smooth and easy tenor around *Jak Szybko Mija Ja Chwile* in Polish, *Du, Du, Liebst Mir im Herzen* in German, and *Cielito Lindo* in Spanish. On the North and East Sides, his playlist often included *I Feel Good* (James Brown), *Blue Suede Shoes* (Carl Perkins), and *You Can't Do That* (the Beatles). By the time the Fourth of July became the Fifth, Norquist had usually expressed in musical terms what it meant to be "mayor for all the people."

Tom Barrett, who became mayor in 2004, brought the tradition to at least a temporary halt. "I love this city and its people too much," he declared, "to ever sing in public." Although he left the tunes to others, Barrett continued the endless round of Fourth of July appearances. Why have so many mayors endured the patriotic marathon every Independence Day? "Because it's a good idea," said John Norquist, "It's an old Milwaukee tradition, and it helps build community." The tradition of the singing mayor has clearly been good for Milwaukee. It happens to be good politics as well.

Minor league baseball at Borchert Field

At Home in the Minors
When Baseball Meant Borchert Field

It didn't have a retractable roof. There was no parking lot for tailgate parties. The foul poles in left and right fields were a tempting 267 feet from home plate, and there was no individual seating, much less luxury boxes. The park had any number of other faults, but baseball in Milwaukee, for more than sixty years, meant Borchert Field.

Built in 1888 as Athletic Park, Borchert Field was a fairly typical nineteenth-century ball diamond. It was shoehorned into a single city block, bordered by Seventh and Eighth Streets between Burleigh and Chambers. The park's wooden benches provided seating for roughly 10,000—more when the deep corners of the outfield were roped off for big games.

The field was used for a variety of athletic events, including football games, boxing matches, and bicycle races, but it is most fondly remembered as the home of the minor-league Milwaukee Brewers. From its debut in 1902 to its demise in 1952, the team played perhaps 4,000 games at Borchert Field, drawing an estimated 8.3 million fans. The faithful were rewarded with eight American Association pennants during the Brewers' long run.

There was plenty of open land near the park in the early years, but by 1900, the sons and daughters of German immigrants had nearly surrounded the facility with closely spaced duplexes. Living across from Borchert required a certain degree of tolerance. Some residents had sweeping views of the action from their second-floor porches, but they also had to put up with congestion, noise, and the occasional home-run ball through their dining room windows.

It was in 1920 that Otto Borchert assumed control of both the Brewers and the ballpark that was later named for him. Raised in a family of genuine brewers, Borchert was a hands-on owner who loved to mingle with the crowd. He was also a shrewd judge of talent. One of Borchert's best catches was Milwaukee's own Alois Szymanski, who found fame (and a lifetime .334 batting average) in the big leagues as Al Simmons.

Simmons was not the only luminary who graced Borchert Field. The Brewers' owner during World War II was Bill Veeck ("As in Wreck"), perhaps the most gifted promoter the game has ever known. To keep the seats filled during the war years, Veeck staged a series of early-morning games for defense workers coming off third shift. Ushers dressed in nightgowns passed out cereal and doughnuts to the crowd, and a pajama-clad band played between innings. Veeck's managers included the legendary Charlie Grimm and, for a single season, Casey Stengel himself.

Bill Veeck's promotions kept the fans coming but, after three generations of watching a minor-league team in a minor-league park, Milwaukee was ready for the bigs. In 1950, after years of discussion, officials broke ground for County Stadium on the city's western outskirts. It was, for Milwaukee, an act of unbelievable abandon; the community's leaders had no assurance of landing a major-league team. "If you build it," they told themselves, "they will come."

And come they did. When the Braves relocated from Boston in 1953, arriving to a hero's welcome, Borchert Field was suddenly superfluous. Otto Borchert's widow sold the ballpark to the City of Milwaukee, who quickly replaced it with a playground. In the early 1960s, the entire site was vaporized for the construction of Interstate 43.

County Stadium served as the home field for some storied teams, including the 1957 Braves and the 1982 Brewers but, after decades of ground balls and grand slams, it ultimately met the same fate as Borchert Field. Familiar pressures—free agency, TV revenue, and the Steinbrennerian appetites of the dominant owners—put intense pressure on small-market ballclubs. Bud Selig, then the team's principal owner, declared that the Brewers were a "fragile franchise" who needed a new stadium just to stay in the game. Local leaders adopted a new mantra: "If you build it, they will stay." In 2001, after heated discussion and endless intrigue, Miller Park opened for business.

With its towering façade and high-tech roof, the new ballpark dwarfed its predecessor, but County Stadium, in its day, was just as much a departure from Borchert Field. The three structures could hardly be more different—a wooden shoebox, an outdoor amphitheater, and a palace of sport—but they share a common lineage. Just as the classic double-play ball went from Tinker to Evers to Chance, baseball in Milwaukee has proceeded from Borchert Field to County Stadium to Miller Park, growing all the while.

Making a Living

Workers pouring molten metal at International Harvester's Milwaukee Works, ca. 1914

Milwaukee and Rock River Canal

Condos on Commerce

Luxury Homes Rise Where Canal Once Ran

There are numerous places in Milwaukee where you can drive on land that used to be water. The list includes Lincoln Memorial Drive, the Menomonee Valley, most of Jones Island, and practically anywhere in the historic Third Ward. The most unusual, in my opinion, is Commerce Street, a riverside roadway just north of the old Schlitz brewery. Once the forgotten spine of an industrial wasteland, the street has become one of the hottest addresses in Milwaukee.

The water that Commerce Street displaced was not a wetland or a lake bed, but a canal dug by a pioneer promoter who hoped it would make Milwaukee the metropolis of the Midwest. The promoter was Byron Kilbourn, founder of the city's West Side and easily the most aggressive of Milwaukee's developers. He arrived in 1834, near the height of an epidemic of canal fever that gripped the entire region.

Canals may seem like antiques today, but they were the eight-lane expressways of their era. At a time when railroads were in their infancy and most overland roads were ruts in the wilderness, canals provided a way to move people and freight over long distances smoothly, safely, and efficiently. The Erie Canal was the undisputed king of America's canals. Completed in 1825, it crossed 363 miles of upstate New York, linking Albany with Buffalo and the Atlantic Ocean (via the Hudson River) with the Great Lakes. The Erie Canal was an overnight sensation, and it earned millions of dollars for the State of New York.

Byron Kilbourn, who had begun his career as a canal engineer in Ohio, was confident of similar success in Milwaukee. With the help of Increase Lapham, a trusted assistant from his Ohio days, Kilbourn chose a route that connected Milwaukee with the Rock River near Fort Atkinson. From the Rock River, he hoped, boats would some day descend the Illinois River to the Mississippi and float all the way to the Gulf of Mexico. The *Milwaukee Advertiser*, a Kilbourn newspaper, ballyhooed the project as a transcontinental artery—"the last connecting link between the Hudson and the Mississippi . . . the *Grand Western Canal*."

Ground for the Milwaukee and Rock River Canal was broken on July 4, 1839. A crowd gathered on the banks of the Milwaukee River near Cherry Street to watch Byron Kilbourn do the honors. His shovel broke on the first attempt, which might have been taken as a sign of trouble ahead, but Kilbourn was undaunted. His crews eventually completed 1.25 miles of canal on the west bank of the river, stretching from McKinley Avenue to a dam just below North Avenue. The dam, designed to provide a steady flow of water for the canal, was an engineering milestone in its own right. A small forest of trees was stacked across the riverbed, leaves and all, and buried under 100,000 cubic yards of gravel.

The dam and the ditch below it were all that Byron Kilbourn ever completed. Kilbourn made enemies easily, and the canal project ran true to form. Other Wisconsinites considered it purely a Milwaukee scheme, and East Siders believed, with good reason, that it was designed largely for the benefit of the West Side. Kilbourn aggravated the jealousies by treating Wisconsin officials in a manner that historian Alice Smith called "overbearing and manipulative." The canal was aborted even before the dam was finished in 1843.

Not to worry. Kilbourn moved easily to the next stage in transportation: railroads. He founded not one but two railroad companies, including a line that paralleled the first leg of his canal. Because it served both the Schlitz and the Pabst breweries, the route was known for many years as the Beer Line.

The stillborn Kilbourn canal was put to good use. Because the dam above it created a reliable source of hydraulic power, the canal spawned Milwaukee's first industrial district. By 1843—three years before the city was incorporated—"the Water Power" was turning the wheels for a tannery, a sawmill, a millwork plant, a planing shop, and a foundry. Six years later there were twenty-five industries on the canal, with a growing concentration of flour mills and tanneries. Milwaukee became a world leader in both fields, and their roots were on the river.

The canal proved to be a temporary attraction. Periodic flooding and a new technology—the steam engine—convinced most riverside industrialists to abandon hydraulic power. The lock at the North Avenue dam was eventually closed, and Kilbourn's dream became a stagnant ditch. In 1884, the city filled it in. Water became land again, and the reclaimed canal was rechristened Commerce Street.

The corridor remained an important industrial district for many decades, but its fortunes faded as the buildings aged and the economy changed. By 1983, the street was so moribund that the State of Wisconsin planned to turn the abandoned Trostel tannery into a medium-security prison. Lovers of old houses, in the meantime, had discovered the marvelous pocket of Victorian homes on the hillside above Commerce Street. They defeated the prison project, reclaimed the homes, and established a vibrant new neighborhood they called Brewer's Hill.

In the 1990s, with more than a nudge from city government, the energy evident on Brewer's Hill spread to Commerce Street. The last structures still standing were recycled. Russ Klisch moved his Lakefront Brewery into the old Commonwealth power plant, and the Gimbels warehouse became the Brewer's Point Apartments. But the emphasis has been on new construction. Anyone who hasn't been to Commerce Street since, say, 2002 wouldn't recognize the place. In a few short years, the street has come alive with some striking examples of contemporary architecture. On Brewer's Hill, what you notice is wooden gingerbread and multi-colored paint schemes. On Commerce Street, it's all sleek modernity—brick, glass, and chrome arranged in angles meant to arrest the eye.

You'd guess that Byron Kilbourn would approve. As taste and money flow down a buried channel of pioneer commerce, his old canal is once again turning a profit.

Frederick J. Miller (center in light vest) with brewery workers

The Father of Miller Time
Pioneer Brewer Built a Lasting Heritage

Companies can't choose their founders, of course—no more than children can choose their parents. If, however, by some genie's wish or angel's intervention, a business could go back in time and create its creator, it would be hard to do much better than Frederick J. Miller. Born with patrician good looks, Miller was ambitious, articulate, and accomplished—someone destined to succeed—but he was also a deeply human individual who observed a careful distinction between making a living and making a life. The values he embraced and the example he provided set the course for a brewery that's still going strong more than 150 years later.

Like most American brewing chronicles, Miller's story began in Germany. The founder was born in 1824 to a middle-class merchant family in Riedlingen, a small town northwest of Munich. His father died when Frederick was only twelve, leaving the family business to his older brother. Forced to choose a trade when he was barely in his teens, Miller gravitated naturally to brewing. He served a ten-year apprenticeship, learning under the tutelage of master brewers in southern Germany and France.

By 1849, Miller was a master brewer himself. At the age of twenty-four, he leased an old brewery attached to a castle just sixteen miles up the Danube River from his hometown. The young man made the most of his new opportunity. One sentence from an 1851 letter to castle officials spoke volumes about Miller's approach to his craft: "My beer in regard to contests was preferred, and rightly so, to that of other brewers."

Committed to quality and determined to provide it, Frederick Miller decided that the New World offered the most promising outlet for his skills. In 1854, accompanied by his young wife and their infant son, he set sail for America. Miller was hardly a penniless immigrant. He arrived in New York with the modern equivalent of $200,000, enough to start his own business and to take plenty of time choosing its location.

After months of investigation, Frederick Miller picked Milwaukee. The decision, in hindsight, was an easy one. Milwaukee was a western boomtown with an abundance of Germans who appreciated good beer, and its winters were cold enough to guarantee a plentiful supply of ice—one of the universal requirements of the trade. In the summer of 1855, Miller took over a bankrupt brewery at Fortieth and State Streets. Its previous owner was Charles Best, whose father and brothers founded the enterprise that became Pabst Brewing.

Frederick Miller succeeded where Charles Best had failed. After sweeping out the cobwebs and refurbishing the equipment, he began to make beer again. His first customers included hotels and saloons in rural hamlets like Wauwatosa and Elm Grove, but the brewer clearly had loftier ambitions. Miller was shipping beer to Chicago during his first year in business, and he followed the rail lines even farther south. By 1860, the immigrant was supplying customers in Memphis and New Orleans, and he had planted the flag in St. Louis, home of the brewery that would become his company's archrival: Anheuser-Busch.

Frederick J. Miller was devoted to the business in its smallest details, but there were limits to his energies. As Milwaukee's larger brewers—Pabst, Schlitz, and Blatz—became national producers, Miller decided to focus on a territory that stretched from Chicago to the mining and lumber towns of the North Woods. That region was more than enough to provide him with a comfortable living. Although Miller never ranked higher than fourth among Milwaukee's brewers, he was an established competitor in a city known for beer, and he walked the streets with the same pride as his friend and fellow beer baron Frederick Pabst.

The brewer's success was shadowed by recurrent tragedy. His first wife, Josephine, died in 1860. A second marriage, to Lisette Gross, lasted for the rest of his life, but Frederick Miller lost seven children in all, from newborns to a teenager named Louisa. Although the immigrant was buoyed by his deep Catholic faith in times of tragedy, he also had the innate optimism of a born entrepreneur. "In spite of all the misfortunes and fateful blows," he wrote in 1879, "I never lost my head. After every blow, just like a bull, I jumped back higher and higher."

Frederick J. Miller jumped back high enough, in fact, to create a business that's still flourishing today. By the time of his own death in 1888, he had established the foundation on which his sons—Ernest, Frederick A., and Emil—built an even larger company, one that saw explosive growth with the introduction of Miller High Life in 1903.

It was on the strength of the High Life brand that the founder's grandson, the charismatic Frederick C. Miller, lifted the company into the national rankings in the 1950s, and it was that stellar showing that attracted the attention of Philip Morris in 1969. Philip Morris revitalized High Life and introduced Miller Lite in 1975, creating with a single brand a category that is now the industry's largest. Today South African Breweries is building on Philip Morris's success to make Miller a truly global player.

It all began with a newcomer who wanted to make the best beer he knew how in a nation that rewarded hard work and an enterprising spirit. But Frederick J. Miller was by no means a one-dimensional workaholic. "Always retain the old, unchanging truth," he advised his German relatives in an 1879 letter, "that happiness is not created by wealth and luxury, but by simplicity, moderation, a pure heart and a peaceful disposition."

It is that warmly human perspective, maintained in the face of repeated heartache, that makes Miller such a compelling figure in the history of American brewing. More than 150 years later, both he and the company he founded still command our respect.

Blatz Brewery advertisement

Brew City

The Story behind the Suds

My family and I were backpacking in northern Ontario a few years ago. On a nearly deserted trail along the shores of Lake Superior, we fell into conversation with a hiker from Ottawa. When he learned we were from Milwaukee, the Canadian scratched his head for a minute and said, "Milwaukee, Milwaukee . . . Oh, yeah—beer."

Never mind that beer hasn't been our most important product since 1890. And ignore the fact that two of our three largest brewers have disappeared. In the popular imagination, Milwaukee is synonymous with beer, and people carry that image with them deep into the wilderness.

Our association with suds is even older than the city itself. In 1840, six years before Milwaukee was incorporated, the Lake Brewery opened near today's Summerfest grounds. Its proprietors, ironically, were Welshmen, and the local German community was not impressed. "Of course," wrote pioneer historian Rudolf Koss in 1871, "their brew could hardly be considered beer in its German sense, but to the Americans this somewhat murky, sweet, and ale-like drink was satisfactory."

The genuine article arrived in 1841, when Milwaukee's first lager brewery was established in Walker's Point. Its owner was a German immigrant whose name is sometimes given as Reuthlisberger—making him sound like a Big Mac with an attitude. Fifteen years after Reuthlisberger opened his stand, there were twenty-six breweries in Milwaukee, nearly all of them owned and operated by Germans. Most were barely micro-breweries by modern standards, but some of the names were familiar: Schlitz, Miller, Blatz, and Best (later Pabst). The foundations of twentieth-century brewing fortunes were in place well before the Civil War.

As the more aggressive brewers embraced technologies like bottling plants and refrigerated railcars, Milwaukee-made beer became a popular export product. Frederick Pabst, a born promoter with a taste for quality, made his family's brewery the largest in Milwaukee by 1868 and the largest in America by 1874. The Schlitz brewery, which came under the Uihlein family's control when Joseph Schlitz died at sea in 1875, ranked second on the local scene, and Valentine Blatz held third place into the 1880s.

Competition intensified as the largest producers widened their leads. By 1885, there were only nine breweries left in Milwaukee, but they produced twenty times more beer than the two dozen firms operating in 1865. Aggressive advertising helped to boost sales. In the 1890s, Schlitz began to call itself "The Beer That Made Milwaukee Famous"— a slogan that has outlived the brewery—and other producers tried just as hard to get their names before the public.

This non-stop promotion cemented Milwaukee's image as a beer capital—despite the fact that other businesses were growing even faster. Although beer was the city's most important product (by value) in 1890, the lead soon shifted to the metal-bending industries: companies that manufactured everything from cranes to concrete mixers and from grinders to gears. None of the metal-benders made consumer products, and therein lies the key to Milwaukee's continuing identification with beer. No one walked down to the corner store for a machine tool or a mining shovel, but beer was sold on the mass market with the help of mass advertising, and so the "amber nectar" remained Milwaukee's best-known product long after it ceased to be the most important.

Milwaukee was eclipsed temporarily by St. Louis in 1901, when Anheuser-Busch became the national sales leader, but Schlitz took over the top spot in 1915. What finally knocked Schlitz off its perch was, of course, Prohibition. The long national drought began on July 1, 1919, forcing Milwaukee's brewers to embrace some novel business alternatives. Schlitz made "Eline" chocolate bars, Pabst turned out processed cheese, and Gettelman manufactured snowplows.

The bad dream finally ended on April 7, 1933—in the middle of another nightmare. The return of legal beer brought joy to the hearts of many Milwaukeeans, but it came back in the depths of the Depression. Although sales grew steadily (with the help of innovations like canned beer), it was not until the prosperous war years that the industry regained its health. By 1946, Pabst was back on top as the nation's leading brewer.

The years since World War II have not been especially kind to Milwaukee's brewing interests. Pabst and Schlitz took turns at the top of the industry rankings for more than a decade, but Brew City gradually began to lose its head. In 1957, Anheuser-Busch outpaced all Milwaukee-based brewers, and the makers of Budweiser have never looked back. Schlitz, in the meantime, after experiencing problems with both product quality and management succession, closed its doors in 1982. Pabst was purchased by a ruthless outsider in 1985 and began a long, slow slide into oblivion; its Milwaukee plant was shuttered at the end of 1996. Many Pabst-drinkers, myself included, felt a deep sense of betrayal when the brewery was abandoned.

Miller has been the brightest spot on the local brewing scene in recent years. Founded in 1855, it did not become a world-beater until Philip Morris purchased the firm in 1969. With the marketing muscle supplied by the tobacco giant, Miller roared into second place on the national scene, particularly after the introduction of Lite beer in 1975.

On the smaller end of the scale, Milwaukee has spawned two high-quality craft breweries—Sprecher and Lakefront—and any number of brew pubs. In some ways, the city has come full circle in the recent past, with a number of small brewers producing quality products primarily for their home markets.

Will history repeat itself? Will the little guys grow into giants and regain the Beer Capital's lost glory? Not likely. I doubt that even Randy Sprecher or Russ Klisch of Lakefront have visions of grandeur dancing in their heads. What remains in Milwaukee, besides the craft brewers and the Rhode Island-sized vats at Miller, is the heritage—and the image. Although its accuracy has faded, our image as Brewtown is both congenial and appropriate. It indicates the historic depth of the community's Germanism and expresses a down-home approach to life that cuts across all ethnic boundaries. No, we're not the brewing capital of the world any more, but beer still runs in Milwaukee's veins.

Falk Brewery

From Beer to Gears

Falk Brewery Was a Pioneer

It's not easy to find. Getting to the Mitchell Park Domes is the easy part. From there you wander west on Pierce Street to S. Twenty-ninth. A quick right, then a left, and you're on a gravel road that seems distinctly out of place so close to the city's heart. The rutted pathway leads down to a cluster of buildings that are doubly distinguished. They are all that remains of one of Milwaukee's great forgotten breweries, and they were also the first home of a company that's still one of the city's great industries.

The brewery was called the Bavaria and, like so many Milwaukee businesses, it began as an immigrant's dream. Franz Falk arrived from Germany in 1848, when Milwaukee was only two years old, and went to work for one of the city's fledgling breweries. By 1856, he had acquired enough confidence and capital to strike out on his own. Falk moved to the country (today's Twenty-ninth Street) and built a sizable complex on a shelf of land overlooking the Menomonee Valley. Within a decade, he was producing 5,500 barrels a year—more than three times the output of the nearby plant that became Miller Brewing.

Beer was a crowded field in Milwaukee. Franz Falk had more than two dozen competitors when he started, but the Bavaria Brewery soon moved toward the front of the pack. Taking advantage of every technical breakthrough, from bottling machines to refrigerated rail cars, Falk made his brewery the fourth-largest in the city, trailing only Pabst, Schlitz, and Blatz. The bluffside complex grew as fast as the company's sales. In about 1870, Falk added a spacious brick stable and an icehouse with walls three feet thick. Remarkably, both buildings are still standing.

By the time of his death in 1882, Franz Falk was worth, in today's dollars, nearly $5 million. His oldest sons, Frank and Louis, continued to build the family fortune. In 1889, they merged the Bavaria Brewery with a smaller competitor, Jung & Borchert, and doubled their output to 120,000 barrels a year.

Then came the fire. On the Fourth of July in 1889, a blaze broke out in the malthouse. It quickly spread to the brew house, releasing an ankle-deep stream of beer into the Menomonee Valley, and then consumed the bottling works. Thousands of glass bottles were fused into a solid mass. Holiday crowds from the nearby beer gardens gathered to watch the spectacle—from a safe distance. The heat was so intense that it shriveled the leaves on shade trees a block away.

The Falks and their partners were back in business within three months. The brewery was rebuilt on a larger scale, and its output was increased to nearly 200,000 barrels a year. But there was another disaster ahead. On August 30, 1892, an overheated drive in the new malt house sparked a blaze that reduced the brewery's major buildings to ashes. When the flames reached the brew house, thousands of gallons of new beer foamed across the grounds.

Two fires in three years were enough to make the weary partners throw in the towel. In October 1893, they sold the business to Capt. Frederick Pabst for $500,000 in stock. The purchase helped to make Pabst the largest brewer in America. The rebuilt Bavaria Brewery continued to operate for a few more years, but Falk lager became a fading memory.

The beer-soaked ground on the Valley's edge gives little hint of its early history today. The old icehouse is the home of an automotive parts business, and the stable houses junked cars rather than beer wagons and draft horses. But the Falk legacy is anything but absent. In 1892, Herman Falk, the fifth of Franz's seven sons, opened a machine shop in one of the vacant brewery buildings. After turning out railway track switches and portable foundries, Herman began to manufacture precision industrial gears—including some of the largest ever made.

As the enterprise grew, it spread out onto the Valley floor, eventually covering sixty acres of filled-in wetland north of the old brewery. The Falk Corporation is there today, occupying land that was purchased by Franz Falk in 1856. Few businesses in Wisconsin or anywhere else can claim such continuity. Falk has also remained the largest gear manufacturer in America—and probably the only firm in the world that shifted, over the course of its career, from beer to gears.

John Gurda

Pfister and Vogel

Milwaukee Leather

Pfister & Vogel Was Once World's Largest Tanner

If you look at the labels in your shoes, you might be surprised to find where they were made. China is probably the leading country of origin, particularly for athletic footwear, but your pumps and penny loafers might have come off the lasts in India, Pakistan, or any number of other developing countries. In the last few decades, American-made shoes have sunk to minority status in most American closets.

It used to be quite different, of course. The United States once had a booming boot and shoe industry, and Milwaukee's role in its growth was pivotal. At the turn of the twentieth century, no city on earth produced more leather. Numerous tanneries had their beginnings here, but the largest by far was Pfister & Vogel. The company traced its roots to 1847, only a year after Milwaukee was chartered, when Guido Pfister opened a leather store near today's City Hall. In the spring of 1848, Pfister and his friend Frederick Vogel built a tannery on the southern edge of the Menomonee Valley. By 1860, it was Milwaukee's most important, with sixty employees and annual sales of $120,000.

Like so many of their fellow Milwaukeeans, the partners were German immigrants. Nearly thirty tanneries were up and running by 1870, and most were owned and operated by Germans. Although Pfister and Vogel were the best-known, newcomers like August Gallun and Albert Trostel were also thriving. As the years passed, Germans were nearly as prominent in Milwaukee's tanning industry as they were in brewing.

It was not simply German skill that made Milwaukee a leather center. The local industry owed just as much to its location near the junction of farm and forest. Farmers in southern Wisconsin and points west shipped thousands of cattle to Milwaukee every year for disassembly. The insides went to packing plants, and the outsides ended up in tanneries. Forests were just as important. In the industry's early decades, the thick bark of the hemlock tree was chipped and stewed to produce tannin, the chemical that turns hides into leather. Northern Wisconsin and upper Michigan happened to have sprawling forests of hemlock.

127

Milwaukee tanners were using nearly 70,000 cords a year in 1892—the equivalent of 350,000 trees.

Although its environmental costs were staggering, the industry became a mainstay of the local economy. In the 1890s and early 1900s, Milwaukee was the largest producer of plain tanned leather in the world. The city's output passed one million hides in 1897 and two million in 1907, enough to make tanning one of the top three or four industries—even more important than beer in some years.

Milwaukee's steadiest customers were the sprawling boot and shoe factories of New England, whose operators valued the quality and durability of the Wisconsin product. Other markets were somewhat more exotic. Cowboys from Tulsa to Tucson relied on saddles and chaps made from local leather, and the nation's farmers and teamsters used horse collars, harnesses, and fly nets that had begun as hides in Milwaukee.

Pfister & Vogel was the acknowledged giant in this gigantic industry. By 1900, the company had four tanneries in the Milwaukee area, and the flagship was its pioneer plant in the Menomonee Valley. P&V's 1848 facility grew to a complex of thirty-eight buildings covering fifteen acres of filled-in marshland at the south end of the Sixth Street viaduct.

Tannery jobs were anything but glamorous. Working with heavy hides and corrosive liquids in a constant stench was not for the faint of heart, but Milwaukee's leather plants provided an economic foothold for generations of newcomers. Pfister & Vogel alone employed nearly 3,600 people in 1919. Germans had been the entry-level workers in the early years. They were followed by Poles, Greeks, and Italians at the turn of the twentieth century. By the World War I era, the doors were opening to African Americans and Hispanics. The Mexican community's pioneers included a group of immigrants who came to work at P&V's Menomonee Valley plant in 1920.

The World War I era proved to be Pfister & Vogel's high point. Milwaukee remained a tanning center, but the soaring popularity of the automobile was an unqualified disaster for the industry. Shoes lasted longer as people walked less, and horse collars and harnesses were rap-

idly becoming antiques. Unsettled postwar markets and booming foreign competition added to the industry's woes. The combined revenues
of Milwaukee's tanneries dropped from $60 million in 1919 to just over
$30 million in 1929. After years of losses, Pfister & Vogel was disman-
tled at the end of 1930. Hides were still tanned at a plant on the Milwaukee River, but other P&V properties, including the Menomonee
complex, were leased for storage and light manufacturing. An industrial giant became an industrial park.

Pfister & Vogel's remnant tanning operation passed through a succession of hands over the years. The most recent owner, United States
Leather, promoted its P&V product as "the Cadillac of Leather," but the
Pleasant Street plant closed in 2000, when the holding company finally
surrendered to what it called "adverse business conditions in the global
footwear market."

Milwaukee still has a handful of tanneries, but none with the rich
history of Pfister & Vogel. The Pleasant Street plant has been razed
for another riverfront condominium project, and the sprawling
Menomonee Valley complex has been converted to offices and housing
—after a thorough cleaning and deodorizing. Immigrants who spent
their working lives handling slimy, foul-smelling hides in the Valley
plant would find the transformation beyond belief. As the memories
fade, only the buildings remain as mute evidence that the world once
walked on Milwaukee leather.

MAY 5, 1886.

State militia inside the Allis Reliance Works

The Cost of the Eight-Hour Day
General Strike of 1886 Led to Bloodshed

We gather each year to remember a tragedy. The date—the Sunday closest to May 5—is always the same, and the place is always the site of a vanished iron mill in Bay View. Even the people are generally the same, a motley bunch that includes union activists, college professors, Bay View residents, and former mayor Frank Zeidler, the group's godfather.

The tragedy we remember took place in the first week of May 1886. For a few days in that long-ago spring, Milwaukee was practically unglued. A general strike, affecting everyone from bakers to brewers, began on May 1 and soon brought the city to a grinding halt. On May 2, nearly 15,000 striking workers massed for the largest parade in Milwaukee's history up to that time. On May 4, as passions mounted, Gov. Jeremiah Rusk called out the militia. One day later, horrified spectators witnessed the bloodiest labor disturbance in Wisconsin's history.

What issue could have aroused such passions? Nothing more or less than the eight-hour day. Milwaukee was a stronghold of the Eight-Hour League agitation that swept the nation in 1886. Most workers of the time routinely put in ten to twelve hours a day, six days a week, for only a dollar or two a day. As the industrial work force grew from a disorganized mass to a well-defined movement, the eight-hour day, without a cut in pay, became its "password and battle cry." A celebrated slogan summed up the movement's core demand: "Eight Hours for Work, Eight Hours for Rest, Eight Hours for What We Will."

The springtime campaign, led by the Knights of Labor, produced a succession of victories. Milwaukee's Common Council passed an eight-hour ordinance for municipal workers before labor's May 1 deadline, and more than twenty private employers followed suit. The general strike of early May was a direct response to companies who refused to adopt the new system. Using both persuasion and intimidation, the strikers soon shut down every major employer in the city, with a lone exception: the North Chicago Rolling Mill Company, a massive iron plant in suburban Bay View.

On May 4, a group of laborers, many of them Polish immigrants, resolved to bring the mill's leaders to heel. Nearly a thousand of them gathered at St. Stanislaus Church, on the corner of Fifth and Mitchell Streets, for a brisk morning walk to Bay View. "Uncle Jerry" Rusk, in the meantime, called out the militia, and the volunteer soldiers began to arrive at the mill shortly after the workers. The crowd greeted them with a shower of sticks, stones, and garbage. A delegation of workers had been inside all the while, meeting with mill executives. When the talks proved fruitless, the strikers served notice that they would return.

On the morning of May 5, a phalanx of workers numbering at least 1,500 marched once more to Bay View. The state militia, who had spent a restless night inside the plant gates, were determined to repel them. One officer issued a blunt order to his troops: "Pick out your man, and kill him." As the crowd surged down Bay Street toward the mill, the militia commander ordered them to disperse. At a distance of 200 yards, it is doubtful that the marchers heard him above their own noise. When they continued to advance, the commander ordered his troops to open fire. At least five people fell dead or dying, including a twelve-year-old schoolboy and a retired mill worker who was watching the commotion from his backyard. The rest of the crowd beat a hasty retreat to the city.

Reactions to the incident varied wildly. Most Milwaukeeans were appalled by the carnage, but many considered the militia's actions justified. "I seen my duty and I done it," crowed Gov. Rusk, staking out his position as a champion of law and order. Others took the shootings as chilling evidence that industrial property was valued more highly than industrial workers.

The Bay View incident ended, for the time being, the campaign to institute the eight-hour day, but it also galvanized Milwaukee's workers. In the fall elections of 1886, the labor-oriented People's Party elected a congressman, several state legislators, and an entire slate of county officials. Although their triumph was short-lived, it was the first tremor in a political earthquake that carried a Socialist, Emil Seidel, into the mayor's office in 1910.

Milwaukee was never the same after 1886. The Bay View shootings were a watershed event in the community's political history, but they also marked the end of the city's civic innocence. The fiction of contented workers laboring under benevolent capitalists vanished with the smoke rising from the militia's rifles. Milwaukee, and the nation, were forced to confront harsher realities, and those realities are by no means resolved today. More than a century after the tragedy, we still meet—to remember a time when people marched and people died for the eight-hour day.

Man working on heavy machinery at Falk Corporation, ca. 1945

Working for Victory

Milwaukee Helped Win World War II on the Home Front

For any American kid raised in the 1950s, World War II was the big one. It was the only conflict that mattered, the epic struggle our fathers won and the victory that sealed our destiny as the strongest nation on earth. The fact that so many other conflicts have intervened —Korea, Vietnam, the Cold War, and a pair of hotter engagements in the Mideast—is sad proof of our inability to coexist without violence, but World War II still has a special resonance.

As the generation that fought it grows smaller by the day, we look back on World War II as a "good war"—the last one fought without ambiguity and without ambiguous results. Motion pictures, monuments, and best-selling books have revived the stories of courage and carnage for a new generation of Americans, but the emphasis is invariably on action at the front. Less dramatic but no less important was the war at home, particularly the massive contributions of America's industries to the military crusade. If the United States had not become "the arsenal of democracy," in Franklin Roosevelt's memorable phrase, the war's outcome might have been tragically different.

In the effort to equip the Allies for final victory, few cities played more important roles than Milwaukee. One statistic underscores the impact of war work on the local economy. Between 1940 and 1944, Milwaukee's manufacturing employment nearly doubled, soaring from 110,000 to almost 200,000. Practically overnight, the city's industries jumped from the forced idleness of the Depression to the breakneck pace of war production. The Falk Corporation, for example, became the nation's leading producer of gear drives for military vessels, including the LSTs that made the landing at Normandy. Millions of Allen-Bradley resistors were used in walkie-talkies, radar sets, and aircraft instrument panels. Tanneries like Pfister & Vogel, Gallun, and Trostel turned out "Army leather" for boots, belts, and rifle straps. Even the breweries got into the act; Pabst shipped its lager to the troops in camouflaged beer cans.

The undisputed giant of Milwaukee's defense industries was Allis-Chalmers. The West Allis company was by far the largest employer in the region, providing work for more than 20,000 people during the war, and those workers turned out an amazing variety of standard products. A-C turbines propelled warships (with the help of Falk gears). A-C flour mills helped to make bread for the troops, and A-C steam turbines generated power for other defense plants. A-C motors drove winches and cranes, A-C tractors pulled field artillery, and A-C construction equipment opened roads and leveled airfields. The one area in which Allis-Chalmers departed from its standard lines involved the Manhattan Project. As a primary contractor, the company produced more equipment, by weight, than any other manufacturer in the country. The end product, of course, was the annihilation of Hiroshima.

Other companies were asked to neglect their standard lines for the duration of the conflict. A. O. Smith, a pre-war specialist in automotive frames, turned out landing gear, bomb casings, and propeller blades. The Heil Company, a leading producer of truck bodies, fabricated torpedo tubes, gun turrets, and smokescreen generators. Hosiery firms made parachute silk. The Vilter Company, better known for refrigeration equipment, manufactured howitzers, and the old Seaman auto body plant produced helicopter parts.

Whatever their specialties, all Milwaukee industries took their place in a chain of production that was impressively local. Allen-Bradley, for instance, sold its industrial controls to Kearney & Trecker and Kempsmith, who sold their machine tools to Allis-Chalmers, who produced the marine turbines that were later connected to Falk gear drives. Dozens of Milwaukee firms might have been involved in a single end product used by the armed forces.

The production effort was hampered, at least in the early going, by a critical shortage of production workers. With the armed forces claiming thousands of factory hands every month, manpower was in short supply, but womanpower helped to make up the difference. Rosie the Riveter was present in Milwaukee, but more important were Wanda the Welder and Katie the Crane Operator. By 1942, women made up nearly a third of Allen-Bradley's shop force, and the proportion climbed to nearly 80 percent at the Allis-Chalmers supercharger plant.

Defense work also opened new doors for African Americans. Blacks had begun to enter the industrial labor force in the World War I era, but their ranks swelled during World War II. At A.O. Smith, for instance, the number of African-American employees soared from zero in early 1942 to more than 800 in late 1943. Some of Milwaukee's black workers were newcomers from Jamaica, recruited by the federal government to man Milwaukee's defense plants. Unprepared for Wisconsin winters, most had returned to their island homes by the war's end.

The war effort involved everyone, and daily life in Milwaukee underwent a host of adjustments. With the advent of gasoline and tire rationing in 1942, public transit ridership reached an all-time high. To ease the strain on buses and streetcars, local employers adopted a system of staggered working hours. As war workers poured into the city from around the state, a critical housing shortage developed. Families who had an extra bedroom were urged to share it with a new arrival. The Hillside housing project, Milwaukee's first foray into public housing, was designed to accommodate war workers. (Political infighting delayed the project until 1948, when it opened as housing for low-income families.) In one of the most telling signs of adjustment to wartime, several Catholic parishes on the South Side began to offer midnight Masses on Saturday night, specifically for the thousands who worked the first shift on Sunday morning.

Too often taken for granted, the war at home was the full complement of the war at the front. In an almost unbelievable feat of coordination, the productive might of the United States was harnessed to meet a military objective. Without the ships and the tanks, the guns and the ammunition, even the gears and the resistors produced on the home front, the Allies would have been forced to fight the war with their bare hands. As a defense capital for the nation, Milwaukee did its part. No less than the troops at the front lines, it was our workers who won the war.

Ice harvesting

Frozen Assets

Ice Trade Saved Winter for Summer's Use

It was a crop that required no seeds. No one had to turn over a single furrow of earth or pull a solitary weed to improve its yield. Year after year, the crop was simply there, available to anyone with the proper tools and sufficient energy, and it began to grow again the moment the harvest was done.

This miraculous crop was, of course, ice. On days when winter begins to seem interminable, it helps to remember that frigid weather was once viewed as a major Wisconsin asset. It was cold, after all, that created the harvest, and without it thousands of households and some major industries would have been seriously inconvenienced.

The local "hard water trade" was established even before the city of Milwaukee. Henry Kroeger, a German immigrant of such generous proportions that he was nicknamed "Ice Bear," was probably the first to enter the business. In 1844—two years before Milwaukee received its charter—Kroeger began to cut ice on the Kinnickinnic River. Within a year, he had moved on to the broader fields of the Menomonee Valley.

One of Kroeger's employees outdid the Ice Bear. John Kopmeier, another German newcomer, struck out on his own in 1849, cutting ice in the Menomonee marsh and then graduating to the Milwaukee River above the North Avenue dam. Kopmeier and his descendants would become the dominant figures in the local ice trade. Their annual harvest reached 4,000 tons in 1878 and climbed to 400,000 in 1900. Much of it was still cut on the Milwaukee River, but the company developed a network of more than 100 icehouses on lakes scattered throughout southern Wisconsin. Known today as Hometown, Inc., the old Kopmeier firm is still selling frozen water, all of it made by machines.

The Kopmeiers and their counterparts adopted methods developed in New England in the 1820s. As soon as the ice was thick enough (a foot was good, eighteen inches even better), horses with spiked shoes were harnessed to single-bladed "ice plows" that had simple outriggers attached. Each blade cut a deep groove in the ice, and the outrigger neatly scribed the line of the next cut. When the entire field had been "plowed," horses and men repeated the process at right angles to their first path, creating an orderly checkerboard of ice blocks that could be sawed or chiseled loose with relative ease.

Workers with long-handled pike poles pushed the ice down open channels to horse-powered conveyors, which lifted the blocks into icehouses on the water's edge. The icehouses were double-walled buildings insulated, like the ice blocks themselves, with thick layers of sawdust—a material of prodigal abundance in nineteenth-century Wisconsin. With enough sawdust applied, ice could last for more than a year in storage.

Since it was seasonal by nature, the harvest tended to attract transient laborers, men who might have cut wood (and made sawdust) in summer and cut ice in winter. They typically had strong backs and the ability to withstand an occasional dunking. Thick planks and sturdy ropes were always close at hand to help rescue men (and horses) who slipped into the drink.

What was hard work for blue-collar Milwaukeeans created an easier life for their more affluent neighbors. In the early years of the ice trade, it was wealthier consumers who bought ice—to cool their food, make ice cream, or add just the right chill to their mint juleps and sherry cobblers.

If ice was a luxury for retail customers, it became a real necessity for two major Milwaukee industries: brewing and meatpacking. Because lager beer had to be fermented and aged at cool temperatures, it was a seasonal activity at first. Most Milwaukee brewers made their beer in winter and stored it for sale in summer, using massive icehouses to keep the kegs cool. Frederick Miller had a better arrangement: a system of brick-lined caves carved into the hillside behind his State Street brewery. Filled with ice, sawdust, and beer, they kept Miller's finest in prime drinking condition all year round. Converted to a museum in 1953, the caves are now one of the high points on the Miller brewery tour.

An abundant supply of ice gave Miller and his fellow Milwaukee brewers an important edge on their rivals in St. Louis and Cincinnati. Producers in more southerly climes occasionally ran out before the summer ended—a situation that would have been unthinkable in Wisconsin.

Ice created a comparable revolution in meat packing. Pork and beef had always been cured in salt, but the advent of ice shifted the emphasis to fresh meat. In 1879, Patrick Cudahy built an icehouse in the Menomonee Valley and instantly had a year-round enterprise. Summer packing, Cudahy wrote, created "an every day business" that was "very profitable, as but very few were engaged in it at that time." Before long, every major packer was slaughtering, packing, and shipping meat with the assistance of ice.

Ice was an infinitely renewable resource—crews could harvest the same field two or three times in a single winter—but it was also a delicate crop. Pollution ruined the urban rivers as a source of ice in the late 1800s (one writer blamed "the warm contributions from the sewers"), and the venue shifted to inland lakes: Pewaukee, Fox, Random, Pike, Geneva, and dozens of others. In the early 1900s, the northeastern shore of Pewaukee Lake was lined with large icehouses conveniently located along the Milwaukee Road tracks.

In the end, it was machines that killed the ice trade. The Pabst brewery installed its first artificial refrigeration unit in 1880, and by 1889 the company had stopped harvesting natural ice altogether. As other brewers and packers followed suit, residential customers absorbed most of the crop. The iceman, with his heavy tongs and leather apron, was a familiar sight in Milwaukee's neighborhoods well into the twentieth century. Machines eventually captured that market as well. Artificial ice replaced the lake variety in local iceboxes, and then electric refrigerators pushed the icebox aside. More than one-fourth of the Milwaukee area's homes had refrigerators in 1936. In the years following World War II, the ratio approached 100 percent.

The icefields are idle today. Snowmobilers and fishing enthusiasts visit the inland lakes, but no one arrives with thoughts of harvest. Once in a great while, a diver will come up with a long-lost pry bar or pike pole, bringing to light a tangible reminder of an industry, and a way of life, that simply melted away.

A Sense of Place

The Court of Honor, 1957

Milwaukee County Courthouse

Justice and Jazz

Cathedral Square Has Been Holding Court since 1836

S ome bring their picnic hampers and cloth napkins for full sit-down
dinners. Others are content to sprawl out on lawn blankets and
pass the Chardonnay. A few just lean their bikes against the nearest tree
and listen. By the time the evening's band swings into action, Cathedral
Square is packed from sidewalk to sidewalk with people who are there
to enjoy the jazz, each other, and a carefree night at the heart of the city.

Jazz in the Park, a free Thursday-night series, has been a staple of
Milwaukee's summer season since 1990, and its setting is a local jewel.
Cathedral Square is a single block of greenery in a district of sleek office
towers, high-rise apartment blocks, and upscale nightspots. The park's
location makes it one of the most urban—even urbane—public spaces
in the region, and it has a feeling of oasis you're more likely to
encounter in New York or Chicago.

Before it was Cathedral Square, however, this distinctive city park
was Courthouse Square. In 1836, one year after Milwaukee County was
organized, Solomon Juneau and Morgan Martin built a courthouse on
the site and presented it to the county. Their gift, which included the
adjoining land, cost the pair roughly $7,000—nearly $140,000 in current dollars. In 1837, the *Milwaukee Sentinel* (a Juneau enterprise)
praised the pair for their "liberality and public spirit." In a surprisingly
modern lament, the paper added that such spirit was "but rarely met in
these days of individual cupidity and self-aggrandizement."

The gift was less generous than it might appear. Juneau and Martin
were the developers of Milwaukee's East Side, and they were locked in a
fierce rivalry with Byron Kilbourn, the West Side's promoter. Anything
that promised to create traffic—a post office, a land office, or a courthouse—was considered money in the bank. Kilbourn himself had
reserved land for a courthouse on N. Fourth Street, near the present site
of Golda Meir School. Juneau and Martin beat him to the punch, but
Kilbourn's intentions survive in the name of Court Street.

The East Side courthouse was a graceful Greek Revival structure that would have looked at home on any New England village green. Measuring only fifty-one by forty-two feet, it was built to village dimensions, but the structure saw heavy use. This hall of pioneer justice was the scene of trials, hearings, harbor meetings, railroad rallies, political gatherings, and even, for a time, a school.

The blocks surrounding the square attracted other kinds of development. In 1847, one year after Milwaukee received its municipal charter, local Catholics began to build St. John's Cathedral. Dedicated in 1853, the church was a towering statement of the Catholic presence in a city that had come to life as a stronghold of Yankee Protestantism.

The little courthouse was hopelessly inadequate to the needs of an aspiring metropolis. In 1836, even before the building was finished, a jail was added to house Milwaukee's first murderers, a pair of liquor dealers who had killed an Indian. (Both escaped before coming to trial.) Wings were added to the courthouse in the 1840s to provide room for other government offices. Soon even they were overcrowded; by the mid-1850s, it was obvious that Milwaukee needed a new seat of justice.

Political infighting delayed the project for more than a decade. Chafing over years of perceived neglect, West Siders demanded that the new courthouse rise on their bank of the river, but East Siders were victorious again. In 1870, ground was broken for a new building directly behind the old one. Dedicated in 1873, the new courthouse matched the self-image of a city on the rise. It was an imposing neoclassical edifice built of Lake Superior sandstone for a reported $650,000—nearly one hundred times the cost of its predecessor.

Critics charged that the structure was overbuilt and underheated. Although it was erected for Milwaukee County, there were simply not enough county courts and related departments to occupy every room. It was only after the city's aldermen and other officials moved in that the courthouse was filled to capacity.

The East Side's twin towers—the county courthouse and St. John's Cathedral—dominated Milwaukee's skyline for years. The municipal offices moved out when the present City Hall was finished in 1895, but the steady growth of county government kept the place busy. It was not until the 1920s that a new building was necessary, and this time West Siders had their way. After years of discussion, the present courthouse at the west end of Kilbourn Avenue was completed in 1931. It would be the last of Milwaukee's neoclassical public buildings. Monumental to the point of heaviness, the courthouse was blasted by Frank Lloyd Wright as a "million-dollar rockpile."

The "old" courthouse on E. Kilbourn Avenue remained standing until 1939, when county officials decided that it wasn't worth recycling. The building was razed, and Courthouse Square—the seat of local justice for nearly a century—finally became Cathedral Square. It survives as one of the smallest but most picturesque parcels in the entire county park system, as well as the oldest. In 1836, only one year after Milwaukee's initial public land sale, Solomon Juneau gave his neighbors their first park. From justice in the nineteenth century to jazz in the twenty-first, Cathedral Square has been in the swing of things ever since.

Pabst family monument at Forest Home Cemetery

"A Cemetery for the City"
History Lies at Rest in Forest Home

It still lives up to its name. Whether you stroll beneath its broad leaves in July or observe its bare bones in January, Forest Home Cemetery is practically an arboretum. This sylvan retreat preserves a generous cross-section of trees native to Wisconsin, but a different kind of history abides beneath its sheltering branches. Forest Home is the oldest active cemetery in Milwaukee, and few graveyards in the Midwest can match its blend of beauty and historical significance.

It was pure necessity that brought the burial ground into being. Nearly all of Milwaukee's first cemeteries were located near the city's expanding downtown, and most fell victim to urban development within a decade of their creation. As graveyards were taken for homes and highways, the bones of uncounted pioneers were unceremoniously heaped by the wayside.

The people of St. Paul's Episcopal Church, a well-heeled congregation in the Yankee Hill neighborhood, decided to end the sacrilege. In 1850, they bought seventy-three wooded acres on the new Janesville Plank Road and declared their intention to develop "a cemetery for the city." Forest Home, as they called their project, was conceived as a "garden" cemetery, a place for "melancholy meditation" that would eventually become, St. Paul's hoped, "a monument of the taste and liberality of the citizens of Milwaukee."

That is precisely what happened. Forest Home was soon Milwaukee's cemetery of choice, and its residents constituted a Who Was Who of local notables. Beer barons and barristers, manufacturers and merchants, publishers and politicians all found a final resting place beneath the tall trees of Forest Home. The cemetery became such a fixture that the city end of the Janesville Plank Road was renamed Forest Home Avenue in 1872.

Although families of more modest means outnumbered them, it was the wealthy who had the most visible impact on the cemetery. From the 1870s through the turn of the century, Forest Home was the scene of a monumental outbreak of one-upmanship. Obelisks, pyramids, crosses, columns, and spheres sprouted like mushrooms after a rain, each larger than the last. As sculptors worked their magic, some sections of Forest Home became virtual sororities of somber stone women, and the cemetery was dotted with one-of-a-kind markers ranging from a massive marble book to a granite steamship.

Liquor wholesaler Emil Schneider won the monument derby in 1894, when his family put up an eighty-four-ton stone pillar capped by the figure of a Greek goddess. But brewer Emil Blatz had the largest structure on the grounds: a 500-ton mausoleum with marble walls and a tile-covered ceiling. Finished in 1896, it stood directly across the road from monuments to the Pabst and Schlitz families, just as brewery-owned saloons once filled competing corners at dozens of Milwaukee street intersections. The cluster is still known as "Brewer's Corners."

A full-time staff of at least fifty people created a splendid setting for the private monuments. In the late 1800s, they developed picturesque ponds, ornate fountains, a brownstone chapel, and seventeen miles of carriageways and footpaths. Flowers absorbed a major portion of their time. Forest Home's greenhouses produced as many as 135,000 plants every year in the 1880s. Most were used on private graves, but thousands adorned the cemetery's common areas. Dozens of beds were laid out with mathematical precision, producing intricate patterns of texture and color in the best Victorian fashion.

All this beauty was not lost on the people of Milwaukee. At a time when most public parks were little more than postage stamps of greenery pasted into teeming neighborhoods, Forest Home was the most lavishly developed and lovingly tended open space in the entire region. It combined the attractions of the Boerner Botanical Gardens, the Bradley Sculpture Garden, and the Mitchell Park Domes in one sylvan package. With the addition of a few deer, a flock of peacocks, and the fish in its ponds, Forest Home was even a small-scale zoo.

Milwaukeeans couldn't get enough of it. On summer Sundays, streetcars bound for the cemetery were packed with families seeking an afternoon of relief from the clamor and congestion of the city. A gatekeeper interviewed in 1888 estimated that Sunday attendance reached a peak of 8,000 people.

There were fewer visitors after 1900, for a variety of reasons. Milwaukee finally began to develop the park system that would win it world renown. Forest Home's sense of splendid isolation faded as the surrounding blocks filled in with homes. Other cemeteries began to challenge the long-time leader for market share during the same years. Although it was eclipsed to some degree, Forest Home did not fade into obscurity. The cemetery continued to expand and evolve, keeping pace with every shift in public taste and industry practice. From "memory gardens" to above-ground crypts, Forest Home offered the full range of twentieth-century burial arrangements, and the cemetery's evolution has continued in a new century. Its age notwithstanding, Forest Home still has nearly twenty-five acres of open land left to develop, enough to last for at least another generation.

Although its future seems assured, it is Forest Home's past that makes this hallowed ground so distinctive. In 1850, a group of Milwaukee Episcopalians decided to create a cemetery for the city. Their vision produced a burial ground that is part arboretum, part stonecutter's museum, and all local history. What lies buried beneath the trees of Forest Home is the foundation of Milwaukee.

Mitchell home

Summer under Glass

Mitchell's Conservatory Preceded Mitchell Park Domes

There are few places more welcoming in winter than the Mitchell Park Domes. Snow and ice may cover the world outside, but the show dome is filled with azaleas in full bloom, cactus plants are flowering in the desert next door, and the tropical dome is, as always, a jungle of sensory delights.

The jungle exhibit is my cold-weather favorite. You step from the bleakness of a Wisconsin winter directly into a pungent paradise of running water, birdsong, and exotic greenery. More than a thousand species crowd the meandering walkways: fragrant orchids, giant hibiscus flowers, date palms, coconut trees, and banyan, bamboo, and banana plants. The air is a musky blend of aromas ranging from pepper to chocolate, and the temperature is a constant eighty degrees even when blizzards rage on the other side of the glass.

Such luxury was once the exclusive province of the affluent few. At a time when the average worker put in nearly sixty hours a week for less than $500 a year, only a handful of Americans had the money, much less the leisure, to create an endless summer and cover it with glass. Milwaukee's Alexander Mitchell was one of the few. In the late 1800s, he developed a private conservatory that was, for its place and time, every bit as sumptuous as the Domes of today.

Mitchell may have been the most successful immigrant in Milwaukee's history. Born in Scotland, he came to the Cream City in 1839 as secretary of an insurance company that evolved into the Marine Bank. Thirty years later, he was president of the Marine and two other flourishing businesses: the Milwaukee Road and Northwestern National Insurance. All three enterprises grew into regional giants, and the Milwaukee Road became, under Mitchell, one of the leading railroads in America.

Mitchell's home grew with his income. Early in the financier's career, he and his wife, Martha, bought a substantial brick house on Ninth Street, just north of today's Wisconsin Avenue. They enlarged the home frequently over the years, at the same time buying and demolishing the homes of their neighbors. By 1876, the Mitchells owned virtually the entire square block. Sitting serenely near its center was their completed mansion, a mansard-roofed showplace that was the envy of less affluent mortals. Remarkably, the building is still with us as the Wisconsin Club.

Even before their remodeling was complete, the Mitchells had created a Midwestern version of the Garden of Eden. By 1870, the estate featured a conservatory complex of six separate buildings containing nearly 9,000 plants under 15,000 square feet of glass. A visiting *Milwaukee Sentinel* reporter (January 25, 1870) was awestruck: "There I saw in one grand, enchanting aggregation the luxuriant exotics of the torrid zone, yielding rich and rare perfume, the beauty and glory of the tropics—rare and radiant specimens of the Creator's adornment of the temperate zone, and those wonderful plants that grow even within the regions of perpetual snow."

The Mitchell conservatory included a tropical house (with banana and pineapple plants), a "vinery" (boasting grapes "as big as plums"), a rose house (with nearly 800 bushes), and an orchard house (filled with peach, apricot, fig, and other fruit trees). There was even a darkened chamber used for the cultivation of mushrooms, which the wondering *Sentinel* reporter described as "a very delicious and dainty dish" prized by "epicures."

Less exotic plants received equal attention. Chief gardener Joseph Pollard cultivated a variety of flowers, including his boss's favorite, the humble carnation. The Scottish tycoon was famously tight-fisted, but he did share his floral bounty with Milwaukee's churches every Easter. Several congregations came to expect annual shipments of lilies, azaleas, roses, and palms from the Mitchell greenhouses.

Alexander Mitchell suffered a fatal heart attack in 1887. He was buried from one of the churches he had filled with flowers: St. James Episcopal, which stood practically across the street from his home. In the banker's buttonhole, as he lay in state, was a single red carnation.

Martha Mitchell spent most of her time at the couple's Florida estate after her husband's death. In 1895, she rented the Milwaukee mansion to a group of well-heeled Germans who had banded together as the Deutscher Club. They finally purchased the property in about 1898 and replaced the conservatory with a dining room and, in true Milwaukee fashion, a bowling alley. There were few other changes until World War I, when a wave of anti-German sentiment convinced the group to change its name to the Wisconsin Club.

As the Mitchell conservatory faded into memory, Milwaukee's Park Commission decided that the community deserved a public facility just as grand. In 1898, the Commission built an elegant glass palace overlooking the Menomonee Valley and filled it with horticultural specimens from around the world. It was Milwaukee's very own zoo for plants, and the site was appropriate: a twenty-four-acre parcel purchased from the Mitchell family in 1890.

Mitchell Park has been the site of Milwaukee's conservatory ever since, but the glass palace was replaced by the present Domes between 1964 and 1967. Strikingly modern when they were new, the conoidal beehives seem less exotic in the twenty-first century, but they continue to draw visitors from around the world.

Their appeal is obvious in every season, and Milwaukeeans can take special pride in the Domes. More than a century ago, our ancestors gazed in wondrous envy at the Mitchell greenhouses on Grand Avenue. Today those splendors are reincarnated in Mitchell Park, and this garden of rich man's delights belongs to all of us.

Milwaukee Auditorium, 1909

If These Halls Could Talk

Milwaukee Auditorium Was City's Parlor

Milwaukee suffers from an embarrassment of riches when it comes to entertainment venues. The Marcus Center, the Pabst Theater, the Bradley Center, the Arena, and the Milwaukee Theatre are practically neighbors in downtown Milwaukee. At the height of the season, when State Street is filled with pedestrians in a hurry, you can't tell if they're rushing to a Bucks game, a ballet performance, or a Broadway show.

We've come to take this variety for granted, but it wasn't always so. Until the mid-1900s, the Milwaukee Auditorium—forerunner of the Milwaukee Theatre—was the city's *only* central gathering space. It served as Milwaukee's front room, the communal parlor we gussied up to entertain out-of-town guests and receive special visitors.

The building was busy from the day it opened in 1909. In its first full year of operation, the Auditorium hosted 188 meetings, 57 trade shows, 44 concerts and dances, 35 conventions, 13 lectures, and 8 circuses. With typical Milwaukee modesty, the building's managers claimed only that it was the "best lighted and ventilated hall in the country."

By the early 1920s, after some judicious improvements, Milwaukee was ready to crow with the biggest of cities. An elaborate brochure described the Auditorium as "The Nation's Meeting Place" in "America's Best-Equipped Convention City." Hyperbole aside, the building was the scene of some red-letter events. In 1916, with war raging in Europe, local Germans staged a week-long "charity war bazaar" in the Auditorium to help the subjects of Kaiser Wilhelm. Its raffles, food booths, concerts, beer garden, and displays raised more than $100,000 "for the relief of war sufferers" in the Fatherland.

One year later, such an event would have seemed positively treasonous. America entered World War I on the Allied side in 1917, and Auditorium gatherings took a decidedly patriotic turn. In 1918, the United Slavs, a group headed by the city's Poles, drew 20,000 to a rally supporting the policies of President Woodrow Wilson, who had made Polish independence one of the war's objectives.

With victory secured in November 1918 (an event celebrated at the Auditorium), Milwaukee turned to less momentous concerns. As the 1920s roared into high gear, the Auditorium was the scene of elaborate trade shows promoting radios, automobiles, and such home improvements as "dripless" electric refrigerators.

There were less salutary gatherings. The Ku Klux Klan rode a wave of intolerance to new heights in the wake of World War I, and Northern cities became its particular strongholds. In 1922, nearly 3,000 Klansmen converged on the Auditorium to hear a message of hatred directed against Jews, Catholics, African Americans, and immigrants from anywhere.

The building was quieter during the depressed 1930s, but it remained Milwaukee's place for civic celebrations. One of the most spirited marked the end of Prohibition in 1933. Nearly 15,000 people jammed the Auditorium for an old-fashioned "Volksfest" featuring sauerkraut, frankfurters and, for the first time since 1919, legal beer.

War clouds soon returned and, once again, not every Milwaukeean was on the right side. In 1935, the Friends of New Germany staged an Auditorium rally in support of Adolf Hitler. Almost 2,000 people, including adults dressed as storm troopers and children in silver shirts, gathered in front of a stage dominated by an oversized swastika. With the bombing of Pearl Harbor in 1941, such rallies became no more than a painful memory.

Year in and year out, the Auditorium hosted political conventions, prize fights, tennis matches, religious revivals, charity balls, bull fights, card parties, wrestling matches, ice shows, banquets, singing festivals, basketball games, bingo tournaments, bicycle races and, of course, conventions—anything and everything that would attract a crowd.

It was in the years following World War II that the city finally outgrew its Auditorium. Demand for an indoor sport facility led to the construction of the Arena in 1950, and nearby blocks gradually filled in with other venues: the Performing Arts (now Marcus) Center in 1969,

MECCA in 1974, the Bradley Center in 1988, and the Midwest Airlines Center (MECCA's replacement) in 1998.

Although it became one facility among many, the Auditorium remained a vital gathering place. I'd bet that every adult in Milwaukee has vivid memories of at least one event in the building. My own initiation came in 1961, when a grade-school classmate and budding Civil War buff dragged me to a Milwaukee Symphony program of music from the 1860s, conducted by Harry John Brown. At thirteen, I was awestruck. More recent memories center around the beer garden at the Holiday Folk Fair, the dog tank at the *Sentinel* Sports Show, and the graduations of all three of my kids from Rufus King High School.

In 2000, the Wisconsin Center District board—owners of the Auditorium, the Arena, and the Midwest Airlines Center—decided to create a new niche for their oldest facility. The result was a radical reincarnation. The undersized Milwaukee Auditorium was reborn as the mid-sized Milwaukee Theatre.

Not all of the exterior changes are obvious improvements, but the new interior is a marvel. The lozenge-shaped main hall was divided into an elegant gathering space on the south end and a two-tiered, 4,100-seat theater on the north. Both spaces exude warmth without compromising the classical appeal of the original design. In memory, the old hall seems cold and cavernous by comparison.

The Milwaukee Theatre project demonstrates that historic landmarks can be not just recycled but reinvented. When the Auditorium opened in 1909, William George Bruce, one of its guiding lights, declared the building a "model structure" that reflected "the liberality and local patriotism" of Milwaukee's citizens. As we grow accustomed to the newest old landmark in our midst, perhaps one day we'll develop the same affection for the Milwaukee Theatre.

Milwaukee's War Memorial Center

Two Birds on a Single Perch

Calatrava Addition Updates Spirit
of War Memorial Center

*Y*ou have to feel a little sorry for Milwaukee County's War Memorial Center. After dominating the downtown lakefront for more than forty years, Eero Saarinen's landmark was thoroughly upstaged by Santiago Calatrava's 2001 addition to the Milwaukee Art Museum. As the Spaniard's sleek new bird preens in the sunlight, its older neighbor seems almost dowdy by comparison.

Middle-aged Milwaukeeans will recall a time when the sun shone just as brightly on the Memorial Center. In its early days, the building drew the same kind of rapt attention that Calatrava's creation has attracted.

The center's story goes all the way back to World War I. In 1918, with Allied victory almost certain, Milwaukeeans endorsed a laundry list of civic improvements to honor the memory of fallen servicemen. The projects included a sports stadium, a riverwalk, a larger auditorium, and a parkway ("Liberty Drive") on the southern lakeshore. Arguments about site, cost, and feasibility doomed the plans. In the end, Milwaukee's only war memorial was a lonely flagpole at the corner of Plankinton and Wells.

Conscience-stricken civic leaders of the World War II era were determined not to let that happen again. In January 1944—long before D-Day or Iwo Jima—three optimistic women's organizations began to discuss plans for a war memorial. Their project quickly developed an irresistible momentum. Even before Japan surrendered in September 1945, the memorial's concept, architects, and fund-raising strategy were all firmly in place.

The center was envisioned from the very beginning as a "living memorial" with a definite emphasis on culture. Planners wanted a place for "art, drama, music, public discussion, and social assembly" that would help Milwaukeeans achieve "a full and fruitful community life." The architect they selected to realize that vision was Eero Saarinen, a

161

native of Finland practicing in Detroit. He was not a particularly safe choice. Saarinen was a master of modernism nearing the height of his powers. (In 1948, he would win the commission for what is probably his best-known structure: the Gateway Arch in St. Louis.) Hiring Saarinen was a clear sign that Milwaukee had no interest in another tired classical temple.

During a 1946 visit to Milwaukee, Eliel Saarinen, Eero's father and partner, attempted to quell the fears of traditionalists. "We are not going to force something on Milwaukee," he said. "We are going to express something that grows in Milwaukee soil. It will be of simple dignity, to infuse inspiration into those who live within its atmosphere."

The first plans depicted a complete campus of buildings: a center for veteran's activities, three halls of various sizes for music and theater performances, and an art gallery. The budget was confidently set at $5 million, and fund-raising began in the summer of 1947. The heart of the drive—Milwaukee's most ambitious to that date—was an aggressive public campaign that included brass bands, patriotic speeches, and door-to-door canvassing. In an effort that lasted less than two months, over $2,200,000 was raised from 60,000 groups and individuals.

Planners hoped to break ground at once and finish the first buildings within a year. They hadn't reckoned with Milwaukee's penchant for bickering over real estate—a habit dating back to pioneer days. Familiar arguments about a site consumed the next six years. One location after another was buried beneath a barrage of neighborhood objections and legal challenges. Milwaukee's postwar housing shortage was a contributing factor; there was stiff opposition to tearing down even a single home for a "highbrow" cultural temple.

By the time the present lakefront site was chosen in 1953, America had been through another international conflict. The project was repositioned as a memorial to those who had given their lives in the Korean War as well as World War II. The vibrant mosaic on the front of the building, created by Milwaukeean Edmund Lewandowski, incorporates the dates of both struggles.

The project was also reduced in scale. True to their Milwaukee roots, the center's leaders were determined to live within their means. Rather than beg or borrow more money, they decided to pay cash for a veteran's center that would also house an art gallery. The "music hall-theater" planned for the present site of the Calatrava addition was postponed indefinitely; it would not come to life until 1969, and then as the Performing Arts Center on the Milwaukee River.

Construction of the downsized Memorial Center finally began in 1955, a full decade after the end of World War II, and crews were at work for the next two years. Nearly on budget and almost on time, the building was formally dedicated on Veterans Day in 1957. The War Memorial Center was unlike anything Milwaukee had ever seen. Four rectangles of concrete and glass seemed to float above the lake, linked at the corners to form an open courtyard enshrining the names of Milwaukee County's 3,000 war dead. The center was an abstract sculpture in its own right, and its pedestal provided a home for the new Milwaukee Art Center.

Given its boldly non-traditional design, the Memorial Center aroused surprisingly little controversy—in public, at least. Some residents grumbled about "that box on the lakefront," but its patriotic purpose tended to discourage criticism. The building won a number of awards for its design team, and local commentators praised it as "startling," "groundbreaking," and "wonderfully monumental architecture."

More recent critics have been less kind, but the War Memorial Center is still an impressive building decades after its dedication. Its significance lies partly in its historical context. The center was Milwaukee's first major piece of modern architecture, and it marked the community's turn from the safety of tradition to broader waters of expression.

Much the same has been said of the Calatrava addition, and there are some intriguing parallels between the two buildings. Both were conceived as works of art that contained works of art. Both were hailed as touchstones of their times, the War Memorial Center ushering in the modern age and the Art Museum addition greeting the dawn of a new millennium. There are even some physical resemblances. The

Memorial Center has always reminded me of a big, blocky bird perched above the lakefront. The Calatrava addition's avian references are even more obvious. With its sunscreen (excuse me—Burke Brise Soleil) fully extended, the structure appears poised for take-off.

But the biggest similarity between the buildings involves their impact on the community's self-image. Civic leaders have promoted the Calatrava addition as Milwaukee's signature building, a symbol of enlightened self-confidence sure to enhance our stature on the national scene. In 1947, when Saarinen's first models for the Memorial Center were unveiled, two Milwaukee women expressed similar hopes. "Gee whiz," gushed one. "Boy, I'll say," her friend agreed. "It's going to be something the whole town can brag about."

North Milwaukee

North Milwaukee No More

Former Industrial Suburb Blurs into North Side

It wasn't much of an experiment. There were no control groups, no scientific samples, no margins of error. I simply stood on the corner of Thirty-fifth and Villard for a half-hour and asked passers-by, "What's the name of this neighborhood?"

The results were, as a genuine researcher might say, inconclusive. Of the nine or ten people I ambushed, about half failed to come up with any name. Two called the area Villard, and one considered it the Northwest Side. But two pedestrians, a burly young man and a garrulous old woman, supplied the correct historic answer: North Milwaukee.

What prompted my experiment was a concern that one of Milwaukee's oldest place names may be fading into oblivion. Year after year, the number of businesses bearing "North Milwaukee" in their names has declined sharply, and in 1994 the North Milwaukee branch library was renamed for Villard Avenue. Patrons, said the librarians, found the name confusing; they thought of North Milwaukee as simply the North Side. I find the loss lamentable. Old names deserve preservation every bit as much as old buildings, and North Milwaukee is certainly one of the most historic neighborhoods in the city.

The community's founder was, surprisingly, a Republican political boss named Henry Clay Payne. In the late 1800s, before the La Follette Progressives dethroned him, Payne was one of an autocratic handful who ran the state Republican Party like a personal fiefdom. The politico also had a day job. In 1890, he became the local manager of the Milwaukee Street Railway, a new firm that would give the city its first comprehensive streetcar system. Payne's boss and chief financial backer was Henry Villard, a New York robber baron who worked in the same stratosphere as the Carnegies and the Vanderbilts. Best known as president of the Northern Pacific Railroad and founder of General Electric, Villard saw the Milwaukee Street Railway as his first step toward a national utility empire.

North Milwaukee was one of Henry Payne's side projects. Two Milwaukee Road lines crossed near Thirty-fifth and Hampton, and Payne decided to make the rail crossing a major industrial center. He bought land in the area, formed development companies, and courted industrial customers. Payne landed several prospects, including a bridge company and a bicycle factory, but the industries needed workers. The transit boss solved that problem by extending a streetcar line across two miles of open land to his would-be suburb. It brought hundreds of factory hands, most of them North Side Germans, to jobs out in the country.

Payne sold lots to the newcomers, and a thriving residential community developed. The Village of North Milwaukee was incorporated in 1897, covering a large rectangle of land bordered by Congress Street, Silver Spring Drive, Twenty-seventh Street, and Sherman Boulevard. Henry Payne named the village's main street for his boss, Henry Villard.

As more industries located along the tracks, North Milwaukee boomed. By 1918, its population had soared to 2,200, and the village became a city. North Milwaukee was a compact and self-sufficient community, with its own sewer and water systems, two schools, a six-member common council, an independent street numbering system, a newspaper, a bank, and (its mayor boasted) eight miles of cement sidewalk.

The City of Milwaukee, enjoying a residential boom of its own, was soon at the suburb's doorstep. Counting on lower taxes, lower utility rates, and better services, a group of North Milwaukeeans launched a campaign for consolidation with the larger city. The result was a pitched battle between "hometowners" and "annexationists" that raged for years. In 1928, finally, voters approved consolidation by a margin of two to one. On January 1, 1929, North Milwaukee joined the city, becoming, with Bay View, one of only two Milwaukee neighborhoods that was once a self-governing municipality.

North Milwaukee today is, like all neighborhoods since the beginning of time, a changing neighborhood. At the turn of the century, North Side Germans made their homes in the community. Today, it is African Americans moving up from the same neighborhoods. Newer residents soon learn the old landmarks: the village hall on Thirty-fifth Street, the ancient oak grove in Smith Park, and the pockets of stately Victorian homes. The community is physically intact, but the old name is apparently dying, and no one seems to mourn.

What's in a name? Ask the residents of Bay View or Walker's Point or Brewer's Hill. What's in a name is identity, a position on the map, a defined space that promotes a sense of belonging. What's in a name is a sense of place, and our older neighborhoods lose that sense at their peril.

Southgate Shopping Center

Requiem for a Shopping Center
Southgate Started the Malling of Milwaukee

You'd never know it existed. When you drive down S. Twenty-seventh Street near Morgan Avenue today, the buildings you notice are a Wal-Mart and a Walgreen's, those two ubiquitous tumors of modern commerce. There's still a movie theatre on the back lot and a Greek restaurant on the corner, but all traces of the original Southgate shopping center have been obliterated.

Southgate was hardly a landmark on the same level as a train depot or a church, but it was significant in its own right. This proto-mall was the first local expression of a national trend that emerged after World War II. "Markets in the meadows," promoters liked to call the shopping centers, and they spread from coast to coast like wildfire.

It was Kurtis Froedtert who brought the flame to Milwaukee. He was best-known as the head of a malting company that supplied tons of germinated barley to the nation's brewers, but Froedtert branched out after the war. In 1949, he unveiled plans for three shopping centers around the rim of the city: Southgate, Westgate (later Mayfair), and Northgate. Southgate would be the first, and Froedtert described it as a commercial breakthrough: "The Milwaukee shopper will be able to make a single, free parking stop at the S. 27th St. center and do all of her day's shopping, comfortably and conveniently, without worrying about her car, the weather outside or carrying her purchases around with her."

Kurt Froedtert had chosen the site with care. Twenty-seventh Street was then Highway 41—the main-traveled road through Milwaukee before freeways—and the parcel lay squarely between the densely settled ethnic neighborhoods of the old South Side and the exploding suburban fringe. He was seeking customers from both ends of the metropolitan spectrum.

After two years of work, Southgate was ready for those customers. The $5 million center was an open-air marketplace, not a true mall; its twenty stores shared a single roof and a canopied sidewalk. The complex covered 105,000 square feet of retail space, and the rest of the thirty-acre site provided parking for 2,000 cars.

Milwaukeeans found Southgate irresistible. The center opened on September 20, 1951—a weekday—and the developers were pleasantly surprised when more than 60,000 people showed up for their "family party." The entertainment was vintage Milwaukee: Polish and Italian folk dancers, polka bands on the blacktop, a visit from Alice in Dairyland, a world champion flagpole-stander and, of course, fireworks.

The traffic jams and hordes of shoppers weren't the only surprises. "Most amazing of all," reported the *Milwaukee Journal*, "was the way the crowd spent money. Milwaukee enjoys a national reputation as a place where almost everybody will go to anything that is free, but almost everybody will stay away if it costs a lot. Nonetheless, a good three-fourths of the persons on the grounds carried bundles—purchases they had made while exploring." The addition of a Gimbels department store in 1954 gave Southgate a genuine anchor. A Krambo grocery store—Milwaukee's largest—opened on the south end in the next year, and the center became a regional magnet.

I can recall those heady days in Southgate's early career. My family lived barely a mile away and, like most South Siders, we were quick to include the center in our shopping routine. I have vivid childhood memories of the pet department at Grant's dime store, the overpowering smell of polish at Hi-Way Shoe Service, and the candy counter near the back door of Gimbels. But my strongest memory is of an unseasonably warm December day when Santa Claus came to Southgate's back lot—by helicopter.

Helicopters and shopping centers both lost their novelty soon enough. As other centers opened—Bayshore in 1954, Capitol Court in 1956, Mayfair in 1958—these prefabricated Main Streets dominated the local retail scene, and the old streetcar-oriented shopping strips lost customers in droves.

Southgate and its peers flourished for nearly two decades, but continued suburban sprawl spawned a new generation of centers that spelled trouble for the pioneers. When Southridge opened in 1970, it was more than ten times larger than the original Southgate. It was also a self-contained, climate-controlled environment, a virtual indoor park with fountains, benches, and even a two-story aviary.

Southgate's owners were not about to go down without a fight: In 1971, they rebuilt their center as an enclosed mall and practically doubled the number of stores. But the trend toward bigger and brassier retailing was hard to buck. As Twenty-seventh Street became a typical American garbage strip—an interchangeable wilderness of towering signs and bright lights—Southgate was nearly lost in the glare. The closing of Gimbels was a body blow, and the advent of "big box" retailers reduced the center to little more than a strip mall. Southgate entered a long, slow slide into oblivion, and in 1999, wreckers cleared the way for—what else?—a Wal-Mart.

I doubt that many Milwaukeeans shed a tear at the center's passing. Southgate was a relic of the recent past, like black-and-white TVs, eight-track tapes, and the garish golden arches of the original McDonald's; it never developed the emotional potency of a Mitchell Street or a Third Street. Its demise was noteworthy nonetheless. In 1951, Southgate represented a brave new world in American retailing. It displaced historic neighborhood shopping districts and was displaced in turn by more novel forms of commerce. The center's brief career speaks volumes about the velocity of change in modern society. From a bold new idea to a fading memory in less than fifty years—where else but America?

Mitchell Street

Mitchell Street Revisited

Historic South Side Shopping Center Still Draws Customers

No, it's not the South Side's downtown anymore. Southgate, Southridge, and other prefabricated centers took care of that years ago. But Mitchell Street remains a Milwaukee treasure. In a difficult time for aging commercial districts, it retains not only the old landmarks but also a measure of its old vitality.

A century ago, Mitchell Street was still the new kid on the block. Until the late 1800s, the South Side's commercial heart was the corner of Sixth Street and National Avenue. Then came thousands of immigrants, most of them Poles, who pushed the borders of settlement farther south. Mitchell Street developed as their downtown. In time the street was called "the Polish Grand Avenue," as important to the South Side as Wisconsin (then Grand) Avenue was to the entire city.

One of the oldest businesses is still there. Goldmann's Department Store (whose slogan could be "If we don't have it, you don't need it") opened its doors in 1896, and customers still come from miles around to buy candy raisins and flannel by the yard. Scores of other establishments followed Goldmann's in the next thirty years. Kunzelmann-Esser ("Nine floors of fine furniture") began to sell brass beds and baby cribs in 1900. Schuster's and Sears built major department stores, and they shared the street with legendary specialty shops like The Grand (women's apparel) and Mayer-Krom (men's clothing). As cobblers and candymakers, banks and bakeries rounded out the commercial mix, Mitchell Street became a magnet for the entire region.

It also became a center of Milwaukee nightlife. In the 1920s, the street had no fewer than five theaters—the Modjeska, the Granada, the Park, the Juneau, and the Midget. Some offered live entertainment as well as movies. The Modjeska, named for a famous Polish actress, was the undisputed queen of Mitchell Street; its vaudeville stage was one of the largest in Wisconsin.

The Depression ended the street's first boom, but the 1930s were not a complete bust. In 1937, when a trackless trolley line replaced streetcar service, local merchants organized what was said to be the largest celebration in the South Side's history. The events included a parade, a street dance (featuring Heinie and His Grenadiers), and non-stop sales that attracted nearly 100,000 entertainment-starved Milwaukeeans.

Mitchell Street was probably at its busiest in the years after World War II. Like most South Siders who grew up in the 1950s, I have clear memories of sidewalks filled from storefront to curbside with shoppers. I also remember the traffic control tower in the Sears parking lot, of all places. During peak periods, a Sears employee barked directions over a loudspeaker to keep all the Nashes and Hudsons moving smoothly.

There was less traffic to direct after 1951, when Southgate debuted as Milwaukee's first "shopping center." As others followed in the next twenty years—Capitol Court, Mayfair, Bayshore, Northridge, Southridge—customers deserted Mitchell Street in droves. The street's merchants were not about to fold. In 1975, they matched city tax dollars with their own funds to create Mitchell Center, a $1.2 million reconstruction. Wider sidewalks, spacious parking lots, and vest-pocket parks gave Mitchell Street the appearance of a semi-mall.

The project made only a semi-impression on the buying public. As sales volume continued to slide, some of Mitchell Street's anchors gave up the fight, including Gimbels (the former Schuster's), Sears, The Grand, and Penney's. By 1985, shopping on Mitchell Street had become, for most consumers, a dying memory rather than a daily habit.

The glass is still half-full, many would argue. Several of the old stand-bys, from Holzman Furs to Paul's Jewelers, are very much in business, and Mitchell Street still has the highest concentration of bridal shops in the state. Newer stores have given the street an increasingly international flavor. Latino businesses are most numerous, among them Lopez Bakery, one of my personal favorites. (The gingerbread pigs can be habit-forming.) The store that once housed South Side Sausage, a Polish-run establishment that made the best kielbasa and kiszka in town, is now an Indian grocery that sells basmati rice and curry mix.

There has also been physical redevelopment. A 1995 project wiped out every trace of the Mitchell Center era; the oversized sidewalks were trimmed back, on-street parking was restored, and the cul-de-sacs were opened again. The Kunzelmann-Esser store has been creatively converted to artist's lofts, complete with pottery kiln, darkroom, and gallery space, and other housing developments are in the works.

Mitchell Street's current look is only the latest in a series of incarnations going back to the 1800s. In more than a century of change, the street has shown an uncommon ability to remake itself over and over again, adapting and evolving to keep pace with its market. In the process, it has become a showcase for some Milwaukee specialties you can't buy—resilience, diversity, and hope. Those qualities, and a good deal more, are on display as Mitchell Street remains open for business.

Fall

Teens jumping rope, 1956

Rufus King

Schools Fit for a King

Fall Buzzer Recalls Beginning of Public Education

Fall, not spring, has always been a time of beginnings for me. Although I left school years ago, autumn still brings with it that sense of quickened tempo and more purposeful activity I remember from childhood. The year ticks through the long, slow sweep of summer and enters again the clockwork world of books and buzzers, lockers and lectures. Not every student enters that world willingly, of course. Mixed with the anticipation is also a sharp sense of sorrow for freedom lost.

The children of early Milwaukee experienced no such emotions. Their year was one long recess, broken by periods of unrelenting labor in field or shop. Schools were not even an afterthought, and parents who wanted an education for their children had to send them elsewhere. Solomon and Josette Juneau, who presided over Milwaukee in the waning years of the fur trade, chose that option—with mixed results. Theresa, their oldest daughter, attended a boarding school in a Detroit convent, and her teachers reported that she was "one of the best and most industrious girls" at St. Clair Seminary.

Narcisse, Theresa's older brother, was another story. When he was no more than fifteen, the Juneaus packed Narcisse off to Green Bay, Wisconsin's metropolis at the time. The bright lights of the big city (population under 2,000) apparently turned the young man's head. When disturbing rumors reached Milwaukee, Solomon dashed off a plaintive note to a friend in the settlement: "I understand that Narcisse is very much dissipated. . . . I am discouraged and used up. I was in hopes that he would do well and I always thought a great deal of him but I am deceived. If you think it best to send him back to me, just do so please." Narcisse finally matured into a responsible adult, even serving a term or two in the Wisconsin Assembly, but his early escapades serve as a reminder that teenagers have tested the parental fences in every age.

Educational opportunities began to multiply in the mid-1830s, when the first land sales brought hordes of Yankee speculators to

Milwaukee. Several hung out shingles as teachers, and the younger children in the Juneau family (there were at least thirteen kids in all) learned their "Three Rs" from people who actually might have had some experience in the field.

One of the more colorful teachers was Eli Bates, a man known for both his peg leg and his fondness for strong drink. Bates, who held classes in the brand-new courthouse, was remembered by one student as "a type of the old-fashioned pedagogue" who "lacked the enthusiasm in his work which would inspire in his scholars the eager desire to push into the realms beyond." Lack of sleep may have been part of his problem, for Bates literally moonlighted as keeper of Milwaukee's first lighthouse, a fifty-foot tower that crowned the eastern end of Wisconsin Avenue. Although it was intended as an aid to navigation, the house was just as famous for the liquor Bates sold there and the card games he hosted. The beacon, his neighbors observed, wasn't the only thing that was lit up every night. There were also one or two tax-supported "village schools" in the later 1830s, but they were scarcely worthy of the name. The buildings were primitive, the books mismatched, and attendance was sporadic at best.

Such was the status of local education when Rufus King came to town in 1845. His credentials were impeccable. King's grandfather, another Rufus, had been both a U.S. senator from New York and ambassador to England. His father, Charles, was president of Columbia University. King himself was a graduate of West Point and a trained engineer, but he gravitated to journalism. "Induced by liberal offers," as a contemporary put it, the young man moved west to take the reins of the *Milwaukee Sentinel.*

Rufus King took an early and active interest in public education. Within a few months of his arrival, the New Yorker was in charge of a study committee that counted 1,781 Milwaukee children between the ages of 5 and 16. Of that number, 356 were in private ("select") schools and only 228 in public institutions, leaving "upward of 1,000 children in the Town of Milwaukee for whose education no adequate provision has yet been made." That, in King's estimation, was scandalous. The editor beat the drum for public education in the columns of the *Sentinel,* but his involvement extended well beyond the newspaper. King was president of Milwaukee's first school board in 1846, and he served three more terms at the helm in the next decade.

By 1857, noted King's *Sentinel,* Milwaukee boasted seven public schoolhouses, all "large, airy, well arranged, and of handsome exterior." The paper added that the teaching corps was "large, carefully selected, and liberally paid," certainly an exaggeration. Stingy taxpayers kept teacher salaries at subsistence levels. In 1859, despite the press of business at the *Sentinel,* King agreed to become Milwaukee's first superintendent of schools. His greatest achievement, according to early school historian Patrick Donnelly, was to impose a semblance of uniformity on a system that had been managed on a strictly free-lance basis.

King left the post after only a year, apparently dissatisfied with the $2,000 annual salary and disenchanted with central-office politics. He went on to more durable fame (and a general's commission) as commander of Wisconsin's fabled Iron Brigade during the Civil War and ended his public career as America's ambassador to Rome.

Rufus King was Milwaukee's educational pathfinder during a period of financial difficulties, public skepticism and, even at that early date, calls for reform. When he arrived in 1845, the area's public schools were an embarrassment. When he left in 1861, they were accepted, if not exactly embraced, as mandatory investments in the community's future. It seems entirely fitting that his name now graces the city's leading public high school. Rufus King didn't have all the answers, but he did have an unshakable faith in the power of education to shape both the character of the individual and the course of society. Every autumn, when the buzzer sounds for school to begin, that faith is just as essential as it was in 1845.

Folk Fair dancers with fans

A Harvest of Heritage

Folk Fair Means a Yearly Return to Roots

In my family, November has always meant two things: Thanksgiving and the Holiday Folk Fair. We celebrate with turkey and all the trimmings on the fourth Thursday of the month, but our holiday season really begins the weekend before at the largest indoor multi-ethnic festival in America. No single event, in my opinion, comes closer to capturing the traditional essence of Milwaukee. The Folk Fair embodies the spirit and the character of a community where heritage is important, where people look back on their roots with unmistakable pride.

The result, on the most immediate level, is a feast for the senses. Nowhere in America will you find a more colorful gathering of costumes, crafts, foods, dances, and music under one roof. But the Folk Fair is even more impressive as a people's festival. It is the work of thousands of Milwaukeeans from nearly one hundred ethnic organizations who want to share their pride and, not incidentally, raise a little money. The participants could be, and frequently are, your neighbors, your classmates, and your co-workers. I have yet to witness a more potent expression of down-home, democratic diversity.

Not surprisingly, ethnic festivals are as old as Milwaukee. Individual groups have been celebrating their heritage since the first German and Irish residents discovered that they were ethnics, an awareness that dawned some time in the 1840s. Multi-ethnic festivals are a more recent development. After a bruising period of intolerance produced by the tensions of World War I, Milwaukeeans decided that it was time to celebrate their diversity again. In 1931, the adult education division of the Milwaukee Public Schools sponsored its first Harvest Festival of Many Lands. The event was basically a pageant featuring the songs and dances of more than thirty ethnic groups.

The International Institute picked up the torch during World War II. Established in 1936 to help new Americans adjust to life in the New World, the Institute worked just as hard to foster intercultural understanding in the community as a whole. In 1943, as part of its broader mission, the Institute sponsored the first Holiday Folk Fair. Held in the auditorium of We Energies' Public Service Building, it was an undeniably modest affair. The food consisted of a single meat casserole, and the entertainment was limited to one Mexican singer and a Polish accordion player. But a seed had been planted.

One year later, the Folk Fair moved to the Milwaukee Auditorium, which enabled the Institute to bring in more food, more cultural displays, and more people. Attendance mushroomed from 3,500 in 1944 to 28,000 in 1953. When the MECCA convention center opened in 1974, the Folk Fair took over the entire complex, and attendance entered the 60,000 range. Today the celebration fills the Exposition Center at State Fair Park.

My own memories of the Folk Fair date to the early Auditorium years. My father and mother traced their ancestors to different nations, he to Poland and she to Norway, and both took their roots seriously; a visit to the Folk Fair was a family ritual every November. What I recall most vividly are wonderful smells, terrible crowds, and the climactic moment of the folk spectacle, when dancers in costumes of every description unfurled a gigantic American flag.

My wife, Sonja, and I have continued the tradition. We started taking all three of our kids to the Folk Fair when they were practically newborns, and they still go with us whenever they're in town. Our family developed a dependable routine over the years. We always attend on Sunday, when the crowds are generally lighter, arriving before noon and staying for the rest of the day.

Our first stop is lunch in the food court. We tend to bypass the more familiar Milwaukee foods—German, Italian, Mexican, Serbian—in favor of dishes less available during the rest of the year, from Swiss cheese puffs to Armenian stuffed grape leaves. When the last crumb of torte has been consumed, we count the number of countries we've "visited" (at least a dozen in most years) and then pass the Rolaids. I'd like to think that exposing our kids to such different foods at an early age curbed any latent tendencies toward finicky eating habits.

Our next stop is the marketplace, a collection of impromptu shops that offers, by definition, the widest variety of international goods you'll find under one roof practically anywhere. We've brought home everything from Finnish glassware to Hmong needlework, much of it modestly priced. When they were younger, our children did the lion's share of their Christmas shopping at the Folk Fair.

When the castanets and the cuckoo clocks begin to blur together, we sit down to watch the folk spectacle. Dozens of groups perform in a dazzling array of costumes, reinforcing Milwaukee's reputation as the folk-dancing capital of the nation. Then it's back to the main hall for more food and a leisurely tour of the cultural displays. By eight o'clock, it's time to head home with our bellies full, our arms full, and our hearts full of appreciation for the world-class diversity that is Milwaukee's birthright.

That diversity is hardly an unmixed blessing; Milwaukee, and America, would probably experience far less friction if we all shared a single ancestry. The Folk Fair demonstrates that our differences can be enriching as well as divisive. What the festival expresses is the fundamental human unity that underlies the widest extremes of ethnic diversity. The message is simple: We are one people with many stories. If only for a weekend, the Folk Fair begins to tell them all.

President Theodore Roosevelt, Milwaukee, 1910

Close Call for Mr. Roosevelt
Campaign Trail Had Its Hazards

every four years, they come in droves. As a swing state in most presidential elections, Wisconsin has become a magnet for Democratic and Republican contenders alike during campaign season. Local airwaves are choked with their ads, and every week, it seems, one of the candidates or a surrogate is either here, about to come, or just departed. Wisconsinites tend to be courteous, for the most part, and the campaign stops pass without serious mishap. No recent visitor, thank goodness, has faced the reception that marred another candidate's appearance in the last century.

That would be Teddy Roosevelt in 1912. Roosevelt had already spent nearly eight years in the White House, from 1901 to 1909, but he became convinced that William Taft, his hand-picked successor, had abandoned the progressive agenda he championed. The former Republican ran against Taft in 1912 as the candidate of the "Bull Moose" Progressive Party. Roosevelt brought his campaign to Milwaukee in October, stopping at the Hotel Gilpatrick on Third Street north of Wells. (The Hyatt Regency now occupies the site.) It was outside the Gilpatrick, on the evening of October 14, that the candidate had a near-death experience.

As Roosevelt was leaving for a rally at the Milwaukee Auditorium, a would-be assassin named John Schrank worked his way to the front of the crowd. At nearly point-blank range, Schrank raised a .38 caliber revolver and pulled the trigger. So much can happen in a split second. Roosevelt staggered visibly as the bullet slammed into the right side of his chest. The crowd gasped and aides rushed to subdue Schrank, but the candidate did not fall. He even had the presence of mind to demand that his assailant be brought forward. "Officers, take charge of him," he said, "and see that no violence is done to him."

Once safely inside his car, Roosevelt unbuttoned his overcoat and put his hand beneath his vest. It came out bloody. "It looks as if I had been hit," he said. But the old Rough Rider refused pleas to cancel his appearance. With a full house waiting, he ordered his driver to proceed to the Auditorium. It was in the dressing room that doctors had a chance to examine the wound. Roosevelt's verbosity, it appeared, had saved his life. The bullet had perforated a fifty-page speech, folded once, that absorbed most of its force. His heavy overcoat and metal glasses case also helped. Even then, the slug had enough velocity to burrow through Roosevelt's pectoral muscle and lodge against his fourth rib.

His wound was seeping, but the warhorse insisted on taking the stage. His introduction could hardly have been more dramatic. The master of ceremonies told the crowd that the man they had all come to see had just been shot. When Roosevelt heard their expressions of disbelief, he opened his coat to reveal a blood-soaked shirt. A number of women screamed. Although in an obviously weakened condition, Roosevelt proceeded to talk for more than an hour. It's unlikely that anyone in the Auditorium paid much attention to the speech. More than once, the Progressive hero seemed to be on the verge of collapsing, and there were repeated calls for him to sit down.

Roosevelt would have none of it. "It takes more than one bullet to kill a Bull Moose," he declared. An eyewitness described the crowd's reaction when this show of machismo finally ended: "The ex-president was given an ovation which shook the mammoth Auditorium to its foundation."

Roosevelt was whisked away to the city's emergency hospital on Michigan Street after the speech. Although X-rays revealed that the wound was "superficial," it was thought best to send the former president to specialists in Chicago that night. The Chicago doctors advised against surgery. The bullet presented no danger, they concluded, and one physician said, "The Colonel can have his choice of carrying the bullet in his body or in his pocket." After recuperating for a couple of weeks, Teddy Roosevelt was back on the campaign trail. His reputation for toughness preceded him.

John Schrank, in the meantime, had Americans scratching their heads. Bavarian by birth and a bartender by trade, Schrank was not an ideologue of any stripe. His sole issue, in fact, was term limits. Teddy

Roosevelt had already served two terms, the gunman argued, and seeking a third was like asking to be crowned America's king. Schrank, a resident of New York City, had trailed his quarry for nearly 2,000 miles before delivering his message in Milwaukee.

Third parties are frequently wild cards in American politics. Teddy Roosevelt trounced William Taft in the November election, but the split in the Republican vote put Democrat Woodrow Wilson in the White House. The Bull Moose returned to private life, turning down the Progressive Party's entreaties to run again in 1916. He died three years later, John Schrank's bullet still in his chest.

Schrank spent the rest of his life in asylums for the criminally insane, first in Oshkosh and then in Waupun. He proved to be as nice as a paranoid schizophrenic could be, even apologizing for the trouble he had caused Milwaukee. The city, in fact, had been nearly as fortunate as Roosevelt. Dallas still feels a collective guilt as the scene of John F. Kennedy's assassination in 1963, and Buffalo was so ashamed when William McKinley (Teddy Roosevelt's predecessor) was killed there in 1901 that they built a towering monument to him in the city's main square.

The Milwaukee incident only burnished the legend of a man who was already an American icon. His bloody undershirt remains prominently displayed at the Theodore Roosevelt National Monument in Medora, North Dakota.

John Schrank became a legend of a different sort. When he died in 1943, after thirty-one years in confinement, Schrank was still remembered as the bartender who almost made Milwaukee infamous.

Early Milwaukee Golfers

Playing under Winter Rules
Milwaukee Golf Waited for Cold Weather

The leaves had already fallen. Halloween had come and gone. Morning frost covered their makeshift course, but in November 1894, a hardy group of duffers met to play Milwaukee's first game of golf. Golf? In November? Definitely. As modern players will testify, the golf bug's bite is deep, and it induces a mania that knows neither cure nor season.

A Chicagoan, Charles Blair Macdonald, was responsible for the initial bite. In 1892, just four years after golf's American debut in a New York cow pasture, Macdonald laid out a crude seven-hole course in suburban Lake Forest. He and his colleagues soon moved to Belmont, twenty miles west of Chicago. The Belmont links became the first home of the Chicago Golf Club and the first eighteen-hole course in the United States.

E.W. Cramer, a transplanted Milwaukeean, was one of the Chicago club's stalwarts. In the first week of November 1894, he invited three old Milwaukee friends down to Belmont for a round of golf: bankers James Ilsley and Grant Fitch and real estate man John Tweedy Jr. It was a case of love at first bite. The trio came home bursting with enthusiasm, and they passed the virus on to fourteen of their closest friends. Golf had found a new home.

Within a few days of their return from Chicago, Ilsley, Fitch, and Tweedy were leading their cronies through the paces of the new game. The group's "course" was an East Side cow pasture, bordered roughly by Locust Street and Hartford Avenue between Downer and Oakland Avenues. (The University of Wisconsin–Milwaukee now covers the northern half of the original "golfing ground.") Homes were already going up in the area; the golfers changed into their knickerbockers and knee socks in a nearby rented room on Frederick Avenue. Tomato cans served as cups on the shaggy greens, and bandannas tied to fishing poles substituted for flags. The group continued to play even after the first snowfall, using red balls to avoid unfindable lies.

As their passion deepened, the players organized the Milwaukee Golf Club, a loose-knit association headed by James Ilsley. The local press soon caught wind of their activities. On November 11, 1894, only a day or two after the inaugural round, the *Milwaukee Sentinel* described the new game for its readers:

> Briefly stated the game consists in driving a small gutta-percha ball around a course provided with a number of holes, generally eighteen, from 100 to 500 yards apart, by means of variously shaped clubs. The game is brimming over with life and jollity and strong excitement. . . . At the bidding of the golfer, this little ball, sometimes called the "gutty," flies over bridges and streams and sand-hills, through thickets of gorse and, alas! sometimes into sand-pits.

The golfers played on the UWM site for another year or two, but greater things were in store. In 1895, a new organization, the Milwaukee Country Club, moved into its first home, a renovated mansion on Lake Drive at Beverly Road, within the present limits of Shorewood. Most of the Golf Club's mainstays were also charter members of the Country Club, and they were soon sharing their obsession with assorted friends and relatives. In 1895, the golfing fraternity laid out a six-hole course on the west side of Lake Drive, and three years later, they enlarged it to nine holes. The original links on Locust were left to the cows, and the Country Club became golf's focal point in Milwaukee.

James Ilsley, a member of the pioneer trio, was the Country Club's first golf chairman. His responsibilities included a flock of 200 sheep that had been introduced to keep the fairways trimmed to playing length. Described as an "erratic" golfer by a contemporary, Ilsley once beaned a sheep with an errant tee shot. The blow was fatal, prompting fellow golfer Francis Keene to pen a commemorative poem:

His graceful swing
Marks everything,
From drivin' down to puttin.'
But he won his fame

At a different game
As a dead sure shot at mutton.

With the surviving sheep keeping a safe distance, play continued on the Lake Drive course until 1911, when the Milwaukee Country Club moved to its present home in River Hills. By that time, golf had begun to shed the elitist image of its early years. (One local reporter labeled the game "a pasture pastime for a handful of wealthy eccentrics.") In 1902, Milwaukee's first public course, a six-hole beauty, opened in Washington Park, and the Lake Park links followed a few years later. As public courses multiplied, the frustrations of the game were available to everyone.

Golf has since evolved into one of the few sports that involves people of all ages as both participants and spectators. The pioneer threesome of 1894 could hardly have imagined what they started. In early November, they braved the cold of an East Side cow pasture to pursue a new passion. More than a century later, that passion is still in full swing.

The Common Good

Police officer helps a young woman, 1900

WHi Image ID 6934

Mayor Henry Maier

Rogues and Reformers
A Menagerie of Milwaukee Mayors

Every four years, the citizens of Milwaukee choose a new mayor. More often than not, it seems, they choose the old one. Other cities might change their leaders the way some people change hats, but not Milwaukee. Once we put someone in office, that person might be there for life.

The mayoral marathons are, relatively speaking, a modern tradition. The city has actually had nearly forty chief executives, all of them men, since the first was elected in 1846, and it would be hard to imagine a more colorful—or more diverse—cast of characters. From rogues to reformers, humorists to machinists, the city's mayors have exhibited the full range of vices and virtues.

One of Milwaukee's most colorful chief executives was also its first: Solomon Juneau. The old French-Canadian fur trader was not chosen for his management skills—an acting mayor did most of the work—but because he was Milwaukee's last link with its wilderness heritage. Although the election confirmed Juneau's status as a community icon, it was not enough to keep him in town. In 1848, the veteran backwoodsman left to found the settlement of Theresa in the wilds of Dodge County.

Juneau's cross-river rivals also took their turns at the helm. Byron Kilbourn, the West Side's founder, won in both 1848 and 1854, and George Walker, his South Side counterpart, prevailed in 1851 and again in 1853. (All of Milwaukee's early mayors served one-year terms. The standard tenure changed to two years in 1876 and four years in 1920.)

Milwaukee was already a city of immigrants by the time Walker took office. In 1850, nearly two-thirds of the population was foreign-born, but Yankees kept a firm grasp on the political reins. Eleven of the city's first fifteen mayors were natives of New York or New England.

They did not set particularly high standards of public service. Graft and corruption flourished on the urban frontier, and Milwaukee's aldermen earned reputations as unscrupulous "tax-eaters." In 1858,

199

Mayor William Prentiss was elected on a reform platform—just twelve years after Milwaukee became a city.

Not surprisingly, it was the Irish who finally broke the Yankee electoral blockade. A Dubliner with the unlikely name of Hans Crocker became Milwaukee's first Irish mayor in 1852, and he was followed in 1863 by Kilkenny-born Edward O'Neill. Although Germans outnumbered the Irish (and everyone else) by a wide margin, it took them much longer to break through politically. It was not until 1884 that Emil Wallber, a Berlin-born lawyer (and prominent Turner), won the city's top office.

A number of other memorable figures occupied the mayor's seat in the 1800s. William Pitt Lynde (1860) was a founder of the Foley & Lardner law firm and the grandfather of Lynde and Harry Bradley, who started the Allen-Bradley Company (now Rockwell Automation). Joseph Phillips (1870) was a French immigrant who committed political suicide by trying to close saloons and dance halls on Sundays. George Peck (1890) won the voters' laughs before he won their votes. A humorist by trade, the creator of *Peck's Bad Boy* had attracted a national following years before he entered the political arena.

One of the most memorable mayors in Milwaukee's history was David Rose, who served for a decade between 1898 and 1910. Corruption was a hardy perennial in the city's political weed patch, but it came into full bloom under "All the Time Rosy." Brothels, gambling dens, and all-night saloons flourished, and votes and favors were generally for sale to the highest bidder.

While David Rose was beating the drum for a "live town," a labor-oriented reform movement gathered steam, and its standard-bearers were all Socialists. Pragmatic and principled, Socialist candidates offered a genuine alternative to the ethical shortcomings of the traditional parties. They reaped the rewards of their non-stop organizing efforts in 1910, when Emil Seidel, a patternmaker by trade, was elected mayor and his comrades took a majority of Common Council seats. The next two years were extraordinarily busy as the Socialists pushed a packed agenda of measures designed to restore public confidence and enhance the public welfare.

Republicans and Democrats ran a fusionist ticket against the Socialists in 1912, sweeping Dr. Gerhard Bading into office, but the die had been cast. Voters liked the frugal, reflexively honest approach of the "sewer Socialists," and in 1916 they made Daniel Hoan, the scrappy Socialist city attorney, their mayor. It was under Hoan that Milwaukee earned a national reputation as one of the best-governed big cities in America. It was also during Hoan's administration that Milwaukee developed its penchant for extended mayoral tenures. Dan Hoan served from 1916 to 1940—a total of twenty-four years—before he was finally unseated by youthful upstart Carl Zeidler.

Zeidler was lost at sea during World War II, and his successor, John Bohn, led a caretaker administration until 1948. When Bohn stepped down, Frank Zeidler, Carl's brother and a devout Socialist, became mayor. He held the office for twelve years before stepping down himself in 1960. Then came the legendary tenure of Henry Maier, whose last name would become virtually synonymous with "mayor." Maier served from 1960 to 1988, a twenty-eight-year record that may stand for all time. He finally retired in 1988, shortly after his seventieth birthday.

John Norquist prevailed in the lively 1988 race to succeed Maier, and he was elected to three more terms without major opposition. The tallest mayor in Milwaukee's history (at six feet seven), Norquist led the charge for greater fiscal discipline and higher public design standards, but his effectiveness was compromised by the disclosure of an affair with a female staffer late in his tenure. Torpedoed by his libido, Norquist left office in 2004. Tom Barrett, a former congressman, won the election that followed, restoring calm to City Hall and reviving the city's Irish mayoral tradition.

Milwaukee's mayors are indeed a study in contrasts, but the more recent models have had one thing in common: long service. In a record that must be unique in urban America, only four chief executives— Hoan, Frank Zeidler, Maier, and Norquist—served for a total of eighty years in the eighty-eight-year span between 1916 and 2004.

Why the longevity? The answer, I believe, lies in Milwaukee's character. We are not a restless people. For better or worse, Milwaukeeans tend to value order and stability over excitement and experimentation.

Back in 1910—the dividing line between before and after in local politics—the Socialists didn't just restore good government; they raised public administration to a standard that was new in American life. As succeeding mayors honored the same standard—or at least a reasonable facsimile—voters rewarded them with long terms. If it's not broke, Milwaukeeans asked, why fix it? Decades later, we're still asking the same question.

Mayor David Rose

When Graft Reigned Supreme

Good Government Was Once a Distant Dream

Milwaukeeans have long considered their public officials an honest bunch—in sharp contrast, they'll tell you, to the sinfulness that abounds ninety miles south. Events of the early twenty-first century challenged that belief. As three aldermen went to jail and several other politicians underwent investigations, Milwaukee felt its halo slipping. The city, it seemed, was no longer holier-than-thou; it wasn't even holier-than-Chicago.

As galling as Milwaukee's ethical lapses were, they paled in comparison with the abuses of the early twentieth century—a time when good government was conspicuous by its absence. The era's kingpin was David Rose, a small-town lawyer who had become a big-city political operative with surprising ease. Elected mayor in 1898, he served, with a single two-year term on the sidelines, until 1910. Rose's official policy toward prostitution and gambling was "containment," but it soon became apparent that vice was flourishing on his watch. "All the Time Rosy" helped Milwaukee become a wide-open town with a thriving convention business.

Vice was just the beginning. David Rose presided during an age of easy virtue, and corruption tainted every aspect of Milwaukee's public life. Aldermen sold their votes for as little as five dollars or a new suit. Industrialists who wanted railroad sidings or street extensions paid extra for the privilege. Saloon licenses were sold for hard cash. The head of the county's House of Correction made a tidy personal profit on chairs produced by his inmates. Elected officials helped themselves to coal, oats, and even horses intended for public use.

Most voters stood idly by as Milwaukee became an ethical desert, but there was always a countercurrent of civic rectitude. A grand jury investigation was launched in 1901. It returned no indictments, but the tide had begun to rise. In 1903, finally, continuing corruption stirred the reform element to action. The Milwaukee Turner Society called a "mass indignation meeting" for September 28 at its hall on N. Fourth

Street. Organized during Milwaukee's heyday as the "German Athens," the Turners had evolved from a gymnastics club with some radical political ideas to a stronghold of civic liberalism.

Long before the speeches began, every seat in Turner Hall was occupied and the aisles were filled to overflowing. More than 3,000 people attended, surely one of the largest crowds in that cherished landmark's long history. The group included many of Milwaukee's movers and shakers. Judge Emil Wallber, the Turners' president and a former mayor, chaired the meeting. The list of notables present included names that may still be familiar today: Pabst, Cudahy, Harnischfeger, Vogel, Johnston, Kieckhefer, and Ilsley.

Both the bluebloods and those with blue collars heard the same message repeated, in German and in English, for more than two hours: Milwaukee was in the grip of "boodlers and grafters," public officials who were fattening themselves at the public trough. David Rose had indeed kept his promise to "put Milwaukee on the map," thundered Rev. Winfield Gaylord: "We now compete for best position with St. Louis, Minneapolis, Pittsburgh, Philadelphia, and New York, for the honor of having the most shameless and unafraid mess of boodlers in charge of our city government."

Before the meeting ended, committees were appointed, resolutions were passed, and the district attorney was urged to bring the scoundrels to justice. Inspired by the outrage evident at Turner Hall, a new grand jury began its work in December, and public investigations were soon nearly continuous. By the end of 1905, 276 indictments had been returned against 83 individuals on every level of government. Convictions followed at a rapid pace. David Rose escaped the dragnet, but District Attorney (and future governor) Francis McGovern called him "the self-elected, self-appointed attorney general of crime in this community."

Good government was not restored immediately. The ongoing scandal tarnished Republicans and Democrats equally, leaving a new party to carry the banner of reform: the Socialists. Led by Victor Berger and drawing their initial support from working-class German wards, the Socialists grew stronger with each election. In 1910, they took over, making a clean sweep of local offices and sending Victor Berger to Congress.

Milwaukee has not been the same ever since, (OK colloquialism) thank goodness. Carrying out the will of the people, Socialists created the squeaky-clean ethical climate that has been a local hallmark for generations. Their work involved much more than restoring an old order; the party of Berger and Seidel, Zeidler and Hoan created an entirely new standard of honesty and efficiency in municipal government. Even the appearance of personal gain at public expense was considered a capital offense. Frank Zeidler, who retired without a pension despite twelve years in the mayor's office, said it best: "Milwaukeeans want their representatives to come into office poor, and to leave office penniless."

Some observers fret that our standards have slipped, that the tattered remnants of Milwaukee's civic virtue have vanished entirely. An opposite case can be made as well. Whenever politicians place private interests above the public good, Milwaukeeans react with outrage. In 2002, for instance, when county officials approved an extravagant pension plan, incensed voters launched a recall effort that produced a new county board and a new county executive.

Such movements demonstrate, with unmistakable force, our sky-high expectations of local government. There have been some obvious ethical lapses, and there is a clear need for both the public and the press to exercise greater vigilance, but it's important to maintain perspective. Like the water in our rivers and the air above our heads, Milwaukee's political climate was once much, much dirtier.

Police Chief Harold Breier

Good Cop, Bad Cop

Milwaukee's Police Chiefs Have Done It Their Way

The hard-boiled cop is a durable stereotype in American popular culture. From the gunslinging sheriffs of old Westerns to the grizzled detectives of the latest TV series, police officers have generally been portrayed as no-nonsense types with broad cynical streaks and little trust in higher authority.

Milwaukee has had the real thing, and more than once—especially at the very top. Until recently, the people who ran the Police Department tended to be self-willed autocrats who practically took the law into their own hands, and not always with the city's best interests at heart. The result was a series of long-running stalemates between the community's police chiefs and its chief executives.

Law enforcement in Milwaukee had been a largely do-it-yourself affair until 1855, when a string of arsons convinced the city to organize a full-time police force. The first chief, serving at the pleasure of the mayor, was William Beck, a German immigrant who had once walked a beat in New York City.

The new chief assembled his force with a careful bow to the city's ethnic complexion; the first officers included five Germans, three Irishmen, and four "Americans." Beck also picked men who could handle themselves on the mean streets of early Milwaukee. "It was always necessary," he said, "to whip a man in a fair fight before you could arrest him." One result was an alarmingly high injury rate. "For the first year," wrote historian Frank Flower in 1881, "the members of the little force were hardly fit for presentation in society owing to black eyes, bruised noses, and sundry other remembrances of arrests effected among the rough classes."

William Beck could hold his own against what Flower called "the ruffianly element." He once collared two burglars by hiding under their hotel bed and overhearing a detailed conversation about their crimes. Beck had less luck with politicians. Mayor after mayor used the Police

Department as a patronage machine, offering jobs on the force as rewards for faithful service. Beck lost his post and won it back again three separate times in a twenty-four-year period. Turnover in the department was high, especially after elections, and professional standards were decidedly low.

As early as 1864, local reformers campaigned for a citizen board that they hoped would put law enforcement above the political fray. The idea languished until 1885, when official corruption was so hard to ignore that the present Fire and Police Commission was established. Police chiefs were given what amounted to permanent terms; unless they demonstrated malfeasance or incompetence in office, the job was virtually theirs for life.

That is precisely how John T. Janssen viewed his position. Appointed chief in 1888, Janssen stayed for thirty-three years—a record that may stand forever. Born in Germany, the chief joined the force at the age of twenty-two and rose steadily through the ranks. When a change in the mayor's office led to his demotion, Janssen took a more lucrative job as top cop for the Milwaukee Road, but he returned to the Milwaukee Police Department as chief in 1888, determined to make it his own.

John Janssen is a paradoxical figure in the department's history. Described by one contemporary as "a Prussian bulldozer," he bore down on certain types of crime and instilled discipline in a force that obviously needed it. He also resisted any and all attempts to politicize his department. The problem was that, over the years, the chief became a law unto himself. "Czar" Janssen took a generally tolerant view of prostitution and gambling, preferring a policy of containment rather than prosecution. He ignored the merit system, appointing and promoting officers entirely at his own discretion, and generally turned a deaf ear to the pleas of clergymen, society women, and reform groups for stricter controls on vice. "You cannot," he once said, "give the people better government than they want."

When David Rose became mayor in 1898, Milwaukee enlarged its already-ample reputation as an open town. With "All the Time Rosy" in the mayor's office and John Janssen in charge of the Police Department, convention-goers never suffered for lack of entertainment. Serious personal crime, however, was relatively rare. In 1906, when Milwaukee had one murder to Chicago's twenty-two and six burglaries to Chicago's 840, David Rose declared, "The larger Milwaukee gets, the better she gets." But Rose, with Janssen's tacit collusion, was taking official corruption to heights his predecessors could hardly have imagined.

The Socialists ended all that. When patternmaker Emil Seidel became mayor in 1910, the reign of graft and favoritism was suddenly over. Janssen and Seidel enjoyed a brief honeymoon. Despite his autocratic style and his tolerance of vice, the chief was an efficient administrator who maintained a generally high standard of public order, and the Socialists felt no particular urge to remove him.

The honeymoon ended during a garment workers' strike in 1910. The Socialists were pledged both philosophically and politically to uphold the rights of the working class, and Seidel was appalled at the rough treatment the strikers suffered at the hands of Janssen's men. He demanded the chief's resignation in no uncertain terms. Janssen replied in three memorable words: "Go to hell." And just in case Seidel misunderstood him, the chief added, "Neither you nor any other mayor can demand my resignation and get it."

Emil Seidel was livid, of course, but he was also powerless. The civil service reforms of 1885 had effectively insulated the Police Department from political pressure, and Milwaukee Socialists found themselves in the rather awkward position of trying to roll back measures that earlier reformers had struggled to enact. Their efforts were fruitless. John Janssen remained in office until 1921, when a stroke diminished his capacities so profoundly that he was finally forced to resign.

It was Janssen's successor, Jacob Laubenheimer, who created the Police Department in its modern form. A non-partisan working with Socialist mayor Dan Hoan, Laubenheimer expanded the force, opened a training academy, initiated radio dispatching, and made his department a model of honesty and efficiency. The mayor and the chief lived across the alley from each other in the Concordia neighborhood on the

West Side, and it is entirely possible that they discussed police affairs while taking out the garbage. By the time Laubenheimer died in 1936, a federal crime commission had singled out Milwaukee's department as the only one in the country worthy of "unqualified endorsement."

A more recent figure, Harold Breier, marked a return to the days of John Janssen. As autocratic as he was incorruptible, Breier ruled the department from 1964 to 1984 with an iron hand, and he did not welcome input from community groups, politicians, or anyone else outside the force. Mayor Henry Maier, who generally shared Breier's passion for the status quo, called the chief "obdurate, bullheaded, and inflexible when it came to any invasion of his statutory powers."

When Breier ended his twenty-year reign—on his own terms, as always—city officials decided that they had had enough of dictators in blue. The rules were changed to limit a chief's term to seven years. Robert Ziarnik retired after five years, and Philip Arreola barely made it to the end of a single term. Then came Arthur Jones, the city's first African-American chief, who took office in 1996 with Mayor John Norquist's active support. Jones soon revealed an autocratic streak oddly reminiscent of Harold Breier, with whom he had had vivid disagreements as an officer. By 2001, amid allegations of racism and insinuations of incompetence, Norquist was calling for Jones' resignation.

He didn't get it, of course, and the issues were far from resolved when both men left office a few years later. In 2003, Nannette Hegerty, who had joined the force in 1976, became one of the few women to head a big-city police department. Hegerty studiously avoided the high-profile power struggles, but her conciliatory posture did not erase memories of past disagreements. From Janssen to Jones, conflicts at the top illustrate that, of all the themes in the long history of the Milwaukee Police Department, politics is perhaps the most important.

General Billy Mitchell

Hometown Hero of the Air
Billy Mitchell Helped Give America Its Wings

The Milwaukee Mitchells are in no danger of being forgotten. The name of this local dynasty graces a popular county park, a street that was once the South Side's shopping center, and our metropolitan airport, as well as a number of buildings and subdivisions. General Mitchell Field may be the best-known of the bunch. For thousands of visitors who come to Milwaukee by air, the first name they encounter is Mitchell.

The airport's namesake—Billy Mitchell—would be a notable figure in any city, but his Milwaukee roots are particularly deep. The general's grandfather, Alexander, was the wealthiest Wisconsinite of his generation. Born in Scotland, the city's first Mitchell ran the Marine Bank, founded Northwestern National Insurance, and established a rail line that would rise to fame as the Milwaukee Road. There were few local enterprises of any consequence that did not bear his imprint.

The tycoon had only one child, John L. Mitchell. Although he nominally worked for the family bank, John spent most of his years as a gentleman farmer with a particular interest in trotting horses. His estate, Meadowmere, was a 400-acre wonderland of fields, forests, and pastures centered around a baronial barn and a twenty-eight-room mansion filled with the finest artwork and furnishings money could buy. Billy, the oldest of John Mitchell's nine children, recalled Meadowmere as the place "where probably the happiest hours of my life were spent and where the home training I was given, the best that could be, will always have its influence in everything I do."

Where was this Shangri-La? In what is now West Allis. The Meadowmere mansion still stands at 5301 W. Lincoln Avenue, much of its original ornamentation intact. The old landmark is now a nursing home called, appropriately, Mitchell Manor.

Billy might have followed in his father's footsteps as a collector of art and a breeder of horses, but he seemed destined for the military life.

When the Spanish-American War broke out in 1898, Mitchell rushed home from school in Washington to enlist in the Army. He was eighteen years old. Spain had surrendered by the time Billy Mitchell's company reached Cuba, but the young man had found his calling. During the next ten years, he served in the occupied Philippines, laid telegraph wire in Alaska, taught cavalry tactics at Leavenworth, and helped to restore communication after the 1906 San Francisco earthquake.

Mitchell climbed steadily through the ranks. In 1912, at the age of thirty-two, he was assigned to the Army's general staff in Washington—the youngest officer ever granted that honor. It was in Washington that the rising star developed his interest in aviation. The Army had purchased its first aircraft—a Wright brothers model—in 1908. Planes were thought to have some potential for reconnaissance, but Mitchell, with utter clarity, foresaw their role as bombers, fighters, and lethal instruments of modern warfare.

He soon had the chance to make his vision a reality. When the United States entered World War I in 1917, Mitchell was given command of a fleet of 1,500 mismatched aircraft flown by British, French, and American pilots, including the famous Eddie Rickenbacker. They were so effective that Mitchell earned a promotion to brigadier general.

With victory secured in 1918, Gen. Mitchell came home and continued to beat the drum for military aviation. In books, speeches, and interviews, he campaigned for an air force separate from the Army and Navy. "Let us be a whole dog," he pleaded, "instead of being the tail of several dogs." Mitchell was an aggressive publicist for his own cause. Practically taunting his peers in the Navy, the general claimed that an airplane could sink a battleship. Calling his bluff, Congress placed a surrendered German dreadnought at his disposal in 1921. After months of preparation, Mitchell's planes dropped their loads on the craft as it lay anchored off the Virginia coast. The ship went down in less than twenty-two minutes. "A bomb was fired today," said an Army ordnance officer, "that will be heard around the world."

Mitchell obviously knew what he was talking about. What marred his campaign was his uncompromising insistence on the *superiority* of military aircraft. "Armies will become auxiliary to air power," he flatly predicted. "The Navy can no longer guard our coasts," he declared. Those were not statements designed to curry favor with his superiors, who reacted predictably. In 1925, Billy Mitchell was demoted to colonel and exiled to an air base in Texas.

He continued to speak out. When two military aviation mishaps cost several lives in 1925, Mitchell issued a 6,000-word statement that built gradually and inevitably to a single, damning sentence: "These accidents are the result of the incompetency, the criminal negligence, and the almost treasonable administration of our national defense by the Navy and War Departments." That was enough for the brass hats in Washington. Billy Mitchell was called back to face a court martial for "conduct of a nature to bring discredit upon the military service."

The tribunal quickly found him guilty. Rather than serve a five-year suspension at half pay, Mitchell quit the Army. He retired to rural Virginia, where, like his father before him, he lived out his days as a gentleman farmer. The crusader died of pneumonia in 1936, shortly after his fifty-sixth birthday.

Only a few years later, Billy Mitchell was completely vindicated. In 1941, Japanese air power made a shambles of Pearl Harbor. In 1945, American air power reduced Hiroshima to rubble. Military aircraft played a pivotal role on every front in World War II. Once considered a pain in the brass, Mitchell was universally hailed as a prophet. In 1946, Congress awarded him a posthumous Medal of Honor. He won more popular recognition in 1955, when Gary Cooper himself starred in *The Court Martial of Billy Mitchell.*

The Air Force has long since achieved parity with the other branches of the armed forces. Billy Mitchell, the well-bred bulldog who led the charge, now lies in Milwaukee's Forest Home Cemetery, a native son who helped give the American military its wings.

Milwaukee Sentinel Building, ca. 1900

All the News That's Fit
Milwaukee's Newspaper Heritage

A.C. Wheeler, Milwaukee's pioneer historian, made a wry observation about the American press in 1861. "There is scarcely an incorporated swamp in the country without its weekly organ. . . .," Wheeler wrote. "There is not a malarious county seat of two houses and a liberty pole, so unhealthy, so abandoned . . . that an editor cannot be found to risk his life, (if not his sacred honor,) in the attempt to make a prosperous city of it with his pen and rollers."

Milwaukee certainly fit Wheeler's stereotype. The community's first newspaper, the *Advertiser*, appeared in 1836, the same year Wisconsin became a territory. There were only a few hundred people in the vicinity at the time, but Byron Kilbourn, the weekly's chief backer, envisioned a metropolis on the west bank of the Milwaukee River. The *Advertiser*'s mission, accordingly, was to sell Milwaukee—particularly its West Side.

The east side of the river, Solomon Juneau's domain, did not suffer in silence for long. In 1837, with major assistance from Juneau, the *Milwaukee Sentinel* was launched. Its stated goal was to serve as "a medium through which the world might become better acquainted with . . . this new and flourishing Territory"—particularly the East Side.

The presence of two papers in one ragtag frontier town made life doubly difficult for both. Harrison Reed, an early *Sentinel* editor, was forced to trade printing and ad space for his family's daily bread. "I had to be editor, printer and purveyor," Reed recalled, "and was obliged to labor about 18 of the 24 hours to meet daily necessities." Conditions at the *Advertiser* were no better.

Although it might have made economic sense, a merger was never discussed. The two papers were separated by politics as well as geography, with the *Advertiser* waving the Democratic flag and the *Sentinel* taking the Whig (later Republican) viewpoint. Partisanship had teeth in

219

those days. The *Advertiser* dismissed a rival editor as "a whiffling, hypo-critical pimp," and the *Sentinel* blasted one public official as "a corrupt and designing knave." Kilbourn himself leveled various charges through the *Advertiser's* columns, calling one opponent "a *base* and *malicious* LIAR" and accusing another of "weakness and imbecility."

As the community grew, new fronts were opened in the newspaper wars. In 1844, two years before Milwaukee became a city, the *Sentinel* became a daily. The *Advertiser* was the *Courier* by that time, and new sheets appeared whenever an editor had access to a press and the prom-ise of advertising dollars. By 1880, there were at least thirty newspapers, both dailies and weeklies, competing for readers in Milwaukee.

As often as not, they were printed in German. Beginning with the *Banner* in 1844, German journals multiplied to serve the city's largest and most diverse ethnic group. In the late 1870s, Milwaukee boasted no fewer than six German dailies. The leader of the pack was the *Germa-nia*, which became a cornerstone of the Brumder family's publishing empire.

The *Sentinel* emerged as the largest English-language daily, but its place was never secure. In 1882, Lucius Nieman, a former managing editor at the *Sentinel*, launched the *Milwaukee Journal*. Although the field was crowded, Nieman's upstart quickly gained ground on its rivals. By 1900, the *Journal's* circulation had passed the 20,000 mark—good enough for first place among the English-language papers. Nieman made the *Journal*, among other things, a champion of high technology, such as it was. His paper was the first in Milwaukee to use typewriters and the first to put homing pigeons into service.

The ethnic press held its own, boosted by the 1888 debut of the *Kuryer Polski* (*Polish Courier*). By 1910, however, Milwaukee's second and third generations preferred to read the news in English. Then came World War I, which practically wiped out the German press. The *Mil-waukee Journal* became a bastion of anti-German hysteria, mounting a witch hunt for friends of the Kaiser and earning the paper a Pulitzer Prize in 1919. In the aftermath of war, the old *Germania* was renamed the *Milwaukee America* and soon breathed its last.

The rabid partisanship of the early years declined after 1900, but it never disappeared entirely. One of the city's most successful papers was the *Leader*, launched in 1911 as the voice of Milwaukee's Socialists. Under Victor Berger's vigilant leadership, it flourished until the Depression, when Franklin Roosevelt's New Deal stole much of the Socialists' thunder. The *Leader* faded in the 1930s and folded completely in the first months of World War II.

By the end of the war, following a long wave of closings and consolidations, Milwaukee was down to two major newspapers: the Hearst-owned *Sentinel* and the employee-owned *Journal*. Their paths converged in 1962, when the *Journal* bought its morning competitor during a protracted strike. It was not, said the *Journal*'s top brass, a merger they had sought. "However," their statement continued, "the *Journal* has an obligation to the people of this city and this state. Permanent passing of a morning newspaper in Milwaukee would result in a serious loss of reader and advertiser service."

Although Mayor Henry Maier never tired of lambasting "the *Journal* monopoly," the two newspapers maintained a lively intramural rivalry. But the public's reading habits shifted steadily after 1962. As a circulation drop entered the free-fall zone, it was the afternoon publications that became the endangered species. In 1995, Milwaukee's major papers merged as the *Journal Sentinel*, appearing every morning.

Scores of newspapers have covered the Milwaukee scene since the *Advertiser* debuted in 1836. Each has added a distinctive voice—cranky or conciliatory, mainstream or minority—to the editorial Babel that typifies and enlivens a free society.

And then there was one.

National Soldiers Home, 1887

An Unsung Home for Old Soldiers
Veterans' Complex Served the Boys in Blue

You might mistake it for a college campus at first sight. Old Main, with its slate roof and brick tower, soars above a cluster of equally venerable buildings. A short walk takes you past the library, theater, chapel, and residence halls, all done in the styles of a vanished century. Stately oaks and maples, some nearly as old as Old Main, dot the surrounding slopes, and a small pond with resident swans adds to the air of repose. The entire campus has the hushed atmosphere of a small school whose students have left for vacation.

Then you notice the gravestones. There are thousands of them, small tablets of blindingly white marble arranged with military precision on the rolling ground behind Old Main. Each bears the rank as well as the name of the person lying beneath, and you realize that this is not a school but a place for soldiers whose long march has ended.

The National Soldiers Home is a familiar landmark to most Milwaukeeans—from a distance. Although the "campus" and its adjoining cemetery stand literally in the shadow of Miller Park, remarkably few people find their way onto the grounds. Old Main and its neighbors are probably the most distinguished and least-visited ensemble of nineteenth-century buildings in the entire Milwaukee area.

The fact that Milwaukee has the Soldiers Home at all is due to the efforts of local women. In the early years of the Civil War, they sent tons of supplies to Union hospitals and knitted a mountain of mittens for Union soldiers. By 1864, it was painfully clear that more was needed. The United States had nothing resembling the Veterans Administration at the time; soldiers disabled by wounds or illness were simply sent home to manage as best they could. Those without families formed a new army of the homeless and the helpless, and their presence was most obvious in the nation's cities.

Led by Lydia Hewitt, the women of Milwaukee resolved to do something about it. In March 1864, they opened a makeshift "Soldiers' Home" in a row of storefronts on Plankinton Avenue, offering "rest and

223

refreshment" to returning Wisconsin veterans. The women's ultimate goal was considerably more ambitious. What they wanted, in the words of one brochure, was "a Home of magnificent proportions, for which we have not marble white enough, . . . a permanent Home for our battle-scarred veterans for all time to come." To raise funds for this great dream, Hewitt and her allies staged a "Great Fair" that ran for ten days in June 1865. Drawing patrons from throughout Wisconsin, the event netted $110,000 for the cause—more than $1.2 million in current dollars.

Although the women had pictured a Wisconsin home for Wisconsin veterans, a larger opportunity surfaced. In March 1865, with the war nearly over, Congress passed a measure creating a national system of asylums for "disabled volunteer soldiers." Why not, reasoned the Milwaukeeans, graft the local project onto the national effort? Offering the Great Fair's revenues as seed money, they convinced federal authorities to locate one of the first three asylums in Milwaukee.

The result was the National Soldiers Home, a complex that came to life on 410 acres a mile west of the city. The first residents arrived in May 1867, settling into converted farmhouses, but new construction was not far behind. Old Main (known today as "Building 2" in bloodless federal parlance) was completed in 1869 from the plans of Edward Townsend Mix, Milwaukee's leading architect at the time. It served as a library, post office, recreation center, and chapel as well as a dormitory for 500 veterans. Other buildings were added as the home's population approached 3,000, and the present complex was virtually complete by the early 1890s.

The Soldiers Home was a self-contained community, and its residents were, to a man, disabled war veterans. Amputees were most numerous, but the complex also served those suffering psychological trauma and drug addiction. Although they could help with farm chores or landscaping projects if they chose, the blue-clad veterans were not expected to work. All were considered "wards of the nation's gratitude" who had earned their lives of leisure. Some joined a home-grown military band or performed in amateur theatricals. Not a few spent time in the home's own beer hall or in one of the saloons that cropped up on nearby National Avenue—a street named for the National Soldiers Home. Most, it seemed, enjoyed the pleasures of merely circulating. "In the Summer," wrote historian Frank Flower in 1881, "those not otherwise inclined can dream away the hours beneath the shades, watching the constant flow of coming and going visitors, listening to the music of the band, or fighting their battles o'er in long drawn yarns told to each other or newer listeners."

Although it was created to serve veterans, the Soldiers Home was a vital resource for Milwaukeeans as well. Until the 1890s, when the city finally developed a park system to match its population, public green space was in critically short supply. With its manicured grounds, winding carriage paths, and scenic ponds, the Soldiers Home was a magnet for hemmed-in urbanites. As many as 60,000 people visited every year in the 1870s, and their numbers peaked on the Fourth of July. From morning parades to evening fireworks, the Soldiers Home was the best place in the region to celebrate America's independence.

No one alive remembers those celebrations in their heyday. The government's focus eventually shifted from residential care for the disabled to medical treatment for all veterans, and the facility's center of gravity moved south to National Avenue, where the Zablocki VA Medical Center now stands. Alone on the hill, the original Soldiers Home lapsed into genteel obscurity. Numerous buildings were torn down, and the structures that were spared are either empty or lightly used today.

Those that remain form a historic district of unusual integrity and an equally uncertain future. The complex will undoubtedly be redeveloped. As the various proposals make their way through the federal bureaucracy, we can all hope that this home for old soldiers will neither die nor fade away but remain what it has been from the start—a landmark for the living.

Milwaukee's Central Library

"Every Person's Gateway"

Public Library System Grew Up With the City

The Milwaukee Public Library has been part of my life since early childhood. When I was growing up on S. Thirty-fourth Street, my whole world lay within a single square mile, a modest realm bordered by my grandparents' hardware store on Lincoln Avenue, Jackson Park on S. Forty-third Street, Blessed Sacrament Church on Oklahoma Avenue, and the Layton Park branch library at 2913 W. Forest Home Avenue.

The library was as far as my siblings and I were allowed to walk when we were old enough to leave the yard. (Drews Five & Dime, in the same block, was an added attraction.) Summertime, especially, was library time, and I plowed through piles of easy readers to remain in Billy the Bookworm's good graces.

By the time I outgrew Billy, the Layton Park branch had moved to another cramped storefront on Forty-third and Forest Home—an important bus transfer corner. My family lived in Hales Corners by then, but the branch remained a regular stop, particularly during my high school years. I must have spent hundreds of hours there between buses on my way home from Marquette High. In those dear, dead days before bar codes and laser scanners, every patron had to enter his or her library card number on a slip in order to check out a book. I used my card so often that the number was hard-wired into my mental circuitry; I'm sure I'll go to my grave remembering 54-13940.

In more recent years, the public library has enabled me to make a living as a Milwaukee historian. From maps to manuscripts, I am absolutely dependent on the collections of the Central Library, especially the treasures stored in the Frank P. Zeidler Humanities Room. Although I visit more often as a patron, I've also been a member of the library board since 1993. I've gotten to know the institution from the inside out, and everything I've learned convinces me that Milwaukee has one of the finest urban systems in the country.

It was in 1878—Milwaukee's own childhood—that the city decided to give library service the same tax support that it was already providing for the street and water systems. Not the same level of support, by any means, but enough to ensure that all citizens had access to a sampling, at least, of their culture's bound heritage.

Although its public incarnation dates to 1878, the library system actually began in the city's infancy. In 1847, just one year after Milwaukee incorporated, a group of book-starved pioneers decided to start a library. It is significant that they met in December, after ice had shut down the shipping lanes—and therefore communication with the outside world—until the following spring. Most of the library's founders were Yankees whose names—Allis, Holton, Vliet, Mason, and others— persist in our street system, if not in our memories. They were uniformly young men who had not yet made their fortunes, and they called their group, naturally, the Young Men's Association. "Regular" members paid a two-dollar initiation fee, while graybeards over thirty-five shelled out five dollars—about $125 in modern currency.

What they received for that sum (and two dollars in annual dues) was unlimited access to a small but growing collection of books shipped from the East. Members could check out one large book (or two small ones) for a period of two weeks, with a one-week renewal privilege.

The Young Men's Association moved its library often in the early years, generally in search of lower rent. Despite a well-received lecture series, the organization was dogged by debt. There was, in the meantime, a rising tide of sentiment for a tax-supported system open to everyone. "If a library is a good thing, and all of us believe it is," the *Milwaukee Sentinel* editorialized, "it is best as a public library."

The breakthrough came in 1878, when the Young Men's Association offered its collection of nearly 10,000 books (a third in German) to serve as the nucleus of a public system. The association's reading room on Milwaukee Street was remodeled, the first city librarian was hired (at $1,200 a year), and the newly public library reopened to a brisk business in July 1878. Two years later, its holdings swollen to 15,000 volumes, the institution moved to the second floor of the new Library

Block, at Fourth Street and Wisconsin Avenue. The reading room there was open to "all well-behaved persons" from nine to nine every day but Sunday, when patrons could enter at two in the afternoon.

By the early 1890s, the collection had mushroomed to 65,000 books, and the reading room was attracting 75,000 patrons a year. Space was soon at a premium. The city decided to solve the problem by building a combined library and museum at what is now 814 W. Wisconsin Avenue. The neoclassical monument opened in 1898, and it was universally hailed as a milestone in Milwaukee's civic progress.

Under the leadership of City Librarian Kate Huston, that landmark was painstakingly renovated in the late 1900s. The Central Library is the hub of a system that includes twelve branches; circulates more than 3,000,000 books, CDs, videos, and other materials; and serves over 2,600,000 patrons a year.

Despite the financial pressures facing all public institutions in an era of scarce resources, the library system remains a pivotal community resource. A public library is the most democratic of all institutions, gathering in one place—whether architectural or electronic—the accumulated knowledge, wisdom, and folly of an entire civilization, and then sharing it, free of charge or restriction, with all who enter.

The Milwaukee Public Library strives to be nothing less than "every person's gateway to an expanding world of information." That is an exalted mission, and it results in a wonderful continuity. There is always a new generation of patrons entering the gateway. When I watch the wide-eyed kids trooping through the Central Library, I'm sure that some of them, too, will look back years from now and proudly say that the library has been part of their lives since the beginning.

Class standing in front of school, ca. 1865

The Roots of Public Education
MPS Was Born to Controversy

Religion and politics have always been sure-fire topics for starting arguments. You can add a third to the list: our public schools. In Milwaukee and elsewhere, they have been the subject of nonstop debate, pitched political battles, and endless experiment. Superintendent after superintendent across the country has been pinned down in the crossfire between would-be reformers, entrenched unions, and taxpayers unwilling to pay another dime.

The controversy reflects, as nothing else can, the critical role that public schools play in a free society. As perhaps the single most important institution shaping the future of that society, they have been, quite properly, a focal point of debate for generations.

In Milwaukee, the earliest discussions concerned the very existence of public education. Although tax-supported schools were legal in the community's pioneer days, they were by no means mandatory. Pioneers typically made their own educational arrangements. In 1835, for instance, Solomon Juneau engaged a schoolmaster to tutor his growing brood. In a tongue-in-cheek letter to a Green Bay friend, Juneau wrote that "natural philosophers" like his were available in quantity: "I think that you might be able to find one in some store in Chicago."

In 1836, Milwaukee opened a "village school," the first to receive public support, but the progress of public education was agonizingly slow. In 1845, nearly a decade after the first bell rang, there were almost 1,800 school-aged children (from five to sixteen) in Milwaukee, and fewer than a third were enrolled in any school, public or private.

The community's leading newspaper found the situation intolerable. In June 1845, the *Milwaukee Sentinel* chided local residents for their neglect of public education: "There is not a public school in Milwaukee, nor has there ever been one. The building used for school purposes in the first district is old, dilapidated, unpainted and half unglazed, without playground or shade, and has not any kind of retreat for the performance of Nature's most private and necessary offices."

The lack of an outhouse was not the only problem. "Out of a school population of 325 children," the *Sentinel* noted, "only about 30 are in school," and the district's annual budget was a paltry $318.

Milwaukee's emergence as a city in 1846 offered the hope, at least, of more adequate facilities for local youngsters. Soon after incorporation, a newly appointed board opened public schools in each of the city's five wards. The first president of the first school board was Rufus King, a native New Yorker and West Point graduate who had arrived in 1845 as editor of the *Sentinel.* King had energy to spare, but not everyone shared his enthusiasm for education. In its first annual report, the board lamented "the too great indifference manifested by parents, and our citizens generally, to the conduct and condition of the Public Schools."

Political fragmentation compounded the problems. Reflecting the sectional rivalries of the frontier years, each city ward constituted a separate school district, and each ward's alderman exercised considerable influence over the selection of principals, teachers, and even suppliers of firewood. It was not until 1907, when school board members were elected in city-wide contests, that the influence of sectional politics waned.

The city's indifference to education persisted for years. Through the Civil War period, fewer than half of Milwaukee's young people attended school in any given year, and teaching conditions were appalling by modern standards. In 1850, male teachers drew an annual salary of only $400 (less than $10,000 in current dollars), and females received only $200 for the same work. In 1859, when Rufus King began his brief tenure as the system's first superintendent, the pupil-teacher ratio was an astronomical sixty-one to one.

Time did not always bring improvements. In 1891, more than fifty years after the first public schools opened, the average primary class had more than sixty-six students per teacher. Administrators also found it hard to remove staff members who were not up to the task. A complaint voiced by the board's president in 1902 had a distinctly modern ring: "It is much easier to appoint an incompetent teacher than to drop one."

Whatever the system's shortcomings, the Milwaukee Public Schools reflected the community's expectations, and for decades those expectations were undeniably modest. Until the 1920s, most children, especially the children of immigrants, left school after the eighth grade, if not sooner, to take their places in the work force. As recently as 1970, fewer than half the city's adults were high school graduates.

Our expectations have grown, particularly since World War II, but the school system's performance has too often moved in the opposite direction. Beset by massive demographic shifts and encumbered by its own bureaucratic inertia, MPS became yet another big-city system in crisis.

The news, however, was never all bad, and I speak as the father of three children who attended MPS specialty schools from kindergarten through high school graduation. Choosing MPS was not a political statement on our part, much less a social experiment; we simply wanted our kids to receive the best possible education in a setting that reflected the diversity of the larger community. Our experience was mixed but positive, as I suspect it would have been at any private institution. In nearly twenty years as active MPS parents, we found substantially more cause for admiration than anger in evaluating our children's schools, and we still pay our property taxes without resentment or regret.

Does MPS have problems? Obviously. Are they insurmountable? Probably not. Perhaps a useful beginning point would be a new awareness of just how much we ask of our children's teachers. When I watch the standouts at work—and they are more numerous than you might think—I feel something approaching awe.

Awe, and complete agreement with George Peckham, Milwaukee's superintendent of schools more than a century ago. In 1894, when he was asked to describe the school system of the far-distant future, Peckham offered a statement of values that is worth repeating today. "It will then be thought," he predicted, "that the work of the bank president, of the busy merchant or of the successful lawyer is not one whit more important than that of the man [or woman] to whom is entrusted the development of thousands of impressionable children."

Mayor Frank Zeidler

Freezing the Common Wealth
Cutting Is Not the Same as Governing

For Wisconsin's public officials, it's been winter for years now. Since 2000, at least, political discourse in the state has been dominated by groups whose agenda can be summarized in a single word: freeze. Freeze taxes or, better yet, cut them and, while you're at it, cut staff, cut salaries, cut services, and cut expectations. At the heart of the insistent cry for "reform," in my opinion, lies a perverse belief that government is a not-so-necessary evil, a system of institutionalized waste that exists to serve pampered workers and selfish politicians.

That cartoonish view of our public life has induced a collective amnesia in the electorate. We seem to have forgotten just what it is our tax dollars support, from clean, safe streets to the streets themselves, not to mention the vital institutions that line them: schools, libraries, fire stations, parks, and all the other elements of our common life.

Those civic necessities are in peril. As the wintry wind of "reform" blows ever harder, officials on all levels are engaged in a dangerous game of chicken, practically daring each other to cut even deeper. Past a certain point, budget cuts are nothing but slow suicide. As services shrink, our common wealth is depleted, and everyone is poorer. Governing, in the process, is replaced by grandstanding, fiscal responsibility by a fiscal free-for-all. True leadership seems to have taken a holiday in Wisconsin. It's as if the Queen of Hearts from *Alice in Wonderland* had seized control. "Off with her head!," she screams, and politicians with even modestly broader agendas run for cover.

We've been here before, of course. As early as 1857, just eleven years after Milwaukee became a city, local aldermen were blasted as reckless "tax-eaters" intent on "waste, extravagance, carelessness and corruption." In the 1880s, a group called the Taxpayers League prevailed upon the state legislature to cap the City of Milwaukee's tax rate. The result was what one historian called "a serious curtailment of municipal activity." Similar pressure was brought to bear during the reform movements of the early 1900s.

In 1938, another group, the Affiliated Taxpayers Committee, demanded what it called "all practical economies in Milwaukee City and County Governments." The committee insisted on deep service cuts and a moratorium on all new programs. Ten years later, yet another taxpayers group petitioned the Common Council to freeze property taxes at their 1942 level, a move that would have crippled essential city services.

Freeze movements are a recurrent theme in Wisconsin politics, but our current winter of discontent seems different in scope and intensity from those of the past. Why such a mania for minimalism? Part of the answer, I believe, is a generalized feeling of economic powerlessness. The costs of health care, college tuition, and gasoline, to name just three variables, have risen without respite, and consumers can hardly use the recall or referendum to bring them down again. Elected officials, on the other hand, are fair game, and disgruntled voters have had a field day. Perhaps their impatience with runaway costs elsewhere has led them to a misplaced attack on government—misplaced because it is ultimately an attack on themselves.

A second force behind the freeze mentality is a surplus of lousy leadership since 2000. When voters in Milwaukee, or elsewhere in Wisconsin, think of their tax dollars at work, they don't visualize the harried health inspector, the overbooked librarian, or the park supervisor trying to cut twice the grass with half the help. They think of grand jury investigations, sex scandals, and prison terms. The misbehavior of a few diminishes the stature of the many, and support for public spending declines with respect for public office.

A third force behind the cut-at-all-costs movement, and the one I find most chilling, is a diminished concern for our common wealth. From the very beginning, one hallmark of American society has been a tension between individualism and community. That tension has been expressed in different ways—competition vs. cooperation, the solitary I vs. the greater We, private rights vs. public welfare—but it reflects our perennial inability to strike an appropriate balance between self and society.

The pendulum has definitely shifted to self in recent years. I recall a cocktail-party conversation with a junior-executive type who was griping about his high property taxes. I pointed out some of the things those taxes paid for, including a world-class park system. He replied, "I'd rather put it in my lawn." I find that viewpoint impoverishing in the extreme. We slowly dissolve into a mass of isolated individuals, each looking out for Number One as the very foundations of civil society crumble beneath us.

A broader, more generous view of government once held sway, and it came to full expression under the Socialists who led Milwaukee between 1910 and 1960. For all their radical rhetoric, the Socialists were public servants first and ideologues second. They understood that government is the most direct expression of our needs and desires as a people. It was on their watch, despite the pressures of depression and war, that Milwaukee was infused with a lively sense of civic possibility.

Although they were famous penny-pinchers, the Socialists also knew that you get what you pay for. Mayor Emil Seidel (1910–1912) believed that Milwaukee could be the most beautiful city in America. "It will cost money," he said, "but what of it? That is what money is for, to be spent for something that is of value. Complaint over the increase in taxes is foolishness. You get more for your money in taxes than in anything else." Unlike a private corporation, Seidel loved to point out, government provides its services at cost, with no expectation of profit.

Mayor Dan Hoan (1916–1940) tried for twenty-four years to build what he called a "better, bigger, and brighter Milwaukee." "The objective," Hoan said, "is to give the best government possible, and, though not necessarily at a low tax rate, at the lowest cost that can be paid."

Mayor Frank Zeidler (1948–1960) also cautioned against down-to-the-bone budgeting. "There is no such thing as cheap government," he said in 1948. "It is better to pay for preventive measures at the start than pay for curative measures later." The underlying purpose of a city, stated Zeidler, was to "create an environment in which a better people can evolve."

We seem to have lost faith in the possibilities implicit in that vision, and it could get even worse. If Wisconsin follows those who march in lock-step loyalty to the bleak agenda of cuts and more cuts, we run some terrible risks. My father-in-law, a much-loved Lutheran preacher who spent most of his career in rural Norwegian congregations, once told of a farmer who tried to wean his pig from food. "I gave him a little less and a little less every day," said the farmer, "and I almost had him weaned. But then he died."

Let's not starve the body politic by cutting off the flow of ideas and energy and, yes, money to the institutions that nourish our life in common. Let us instead feed the traditions that speak to the ancient human need for community. We can cut everything from garbage pick-up to floral plantings in pursuit of lower tax levies and less grumpy voters, but what we risk is the most frightening bankruptcy of all—the bankruptcy of our civic souls.

During various hard times in the past, the unemployed have carried signs that read, "Will Work for Food." What we need today is yard after yard sprouting signs that read, "Will Pay for Services." And we need public officials who will embrace the hard work of public enterprise. We need men and women who can breathe new life into a notion as timeless as it is timely: Government, in the end, is all of us.

Celebrations!

Beer and sweet corn in Milwaukee, 1968

Schlitz Park

Beer, Bands, and Balloon Rides

Milwaukee's Summer Gardens Offered Something for All

There's nothing quite like them in modern Milwaukee. To imagine a nineteenth-century beer garden in all its glory, you'd have to begin with a huge family picnic; add the holiday mood of an ethnic festival; throw in the music of Strauss and Sousa; sprinkle it all with a touch of carnival midway and a trace of zoo; then set the whole package in the leafy splendor of a carefully landscaped park—and, while you're at it, don't forget the beer.

Milwaukee's beer gardens provided all-in-one summer entertainment for every class of residents. The first opened in 1844, two years before Milwaukee received its city charter. Situated on the east bank of the river near Cherry Street, Ludwig's Garden won praise for its "well-cultivated flowers, extensive promenades, rustic bowers, and a beautiful view." By the late 1800s, there were nearly a dozen similar parks. Local author Charles King described the abundance of "summer breathing places" in 1891: "All the outskirts of the city, north, west, south, are dotted with . . . gardens where the people dance, sing, drink their beer and are rationally happy."

Some of the biggest and busiest hangouts for the "rationally happy" were owned by local breweries. King considered Schlitz Park, near Eighth and Walnut Streets, "the most cosmopolitan of resorts," a place so European that it reminded him of Vienna. The park's Sunday programs ranged from light opera to diving horses, and a rustic wooden tower offered sweeping views of the entire city.

The Pabst brewery owned two facilities. The best-known was a resort on the lake bluff in Whitefish Bay at the foot of today's Henry Clay Street. Thousands of pleasure-seekers filled the park on summer weekends for planked whitefish dinners, band concerts, and Ferris wheel rides. Pabst's in-town alternative was located on Third Street and Garfield Avenue. Once a shooting range operated by a German rifle club, Pabst Park became a stationary carnival, with a roller coaster, an ornate carousel, and a fun house called Katzenjammer Castle.

Miller Garden crowned the bluff above Fred Miller's brewery at the city's western limits. Described by the *Milwaukee Sentinel* as "a very pleasing place to while away the hours of a scorching afternoon," its attractions included a music pavilion, a bowling alley, and sumptuous food prepared by the brewer's wife, Lisette.

Other beer gardens were well within the urban fringe. The Milwaukee Garden covered the block between Fourteenth and Fifteenth Streets north of State—the heart of an intensely German neighborhood. In addition to the usual bandstands, bars, and bowers, the park featured a "menagerie" whose stars were a couple of young alligators. National Park, southwest of Twenty-seventh Street and National Avenue, offered even more amenities: a baseball diamond, a dancing pavilion, a roller coaster, and a half-mile track that drew some of the fastest horses in the region. For one season, at least, the garden even offered balloon ascensions "under the direction of Prof. Haydn."

Whatever their locations or their attractions, Milwaukee's beer gardens had much in common. First of all, they catered to residents of every age. Solitary drinkers would not have felt particularly at home in the family-centered environment of most gardens. From the bands they hired to the midways they built, managers tried to provide something for everyone from small children to senior citizens.

The gardens were also overwhelmingly European—a fairly safe description of most social activities in nineteenth-century Milwaukee. The custom of drinking beer beneath the open skies was imported from Germany, but other immigrants obviously found it congenial. In 1886, the *Sentinel* described the beer-garden gatherings of a single Sunday afternoon. Nearly 3,000 Norwegians, reported the paper, trooped out to National Park for a group picnic, complete with speeches, recitations, dancing, and singing, all of which was enjoyed immensely by "the flaxen-haired people." The North Side Turners, meanwhile, were putting on a gymnastics exhibition at Schlitz Park, followed by a band concert. The Vorwaerts Turners offered a similar program at Lueddemann's-on-the-Lake, and the South Side Turners showed off their prowess at a beer garden on Greenfield Avenue. Rose Hill Park, near Sixteenth Street and Forest Home Avenue, drew hundreds of recent Polish immigrants to a gathering of the Polish National Alliance. Across town, the Milwaukee Garden was filled with German societies enjoying "würstle, knöchle, späzle and sauerkraut" with their beer.

Not every Milwaukeean found such activities uplifting. Yankees with more constrained views of Sabbath observance were scandalized by the sight of men, women, and children spending their Sunday afternoons in the presence of beer. "Sunday orgies," one patriot called the assemblies.

It was good government, ironically, that hastened the end of this Milwaukee institution. In 1890, after years of discussion, the city finally got into the park business on a scale befitting its size. It didn't take local residents long to figure out that public parks had most of the amenities of private gardens, without the admission fees. As revenues plummeted, a number of private parks were purchased for public use. In their current incarnations, those parks include Carver (Schlitz), Rose (Pabst), Lake (Lueddemann's), Hubbard (another Lueddemann's), Jackson (Reynolds), and Pleasant Valley (Blatz). An even larger number of private parks were sold to developers and then subdivided. By the time Prohibition drove the last nail into their coffins in 1919, beer gardens had already become a memory for most residents.

With their demise, Milwaukee lost some of its most distinctive landmarks and most appealing reasons to stay outdoors on a summer night. Even in these days of central air and automatic ice machines, it's not hard to feel that we're poorer for their passing.

Fourth of July

An Old-Fashioned Fourth of July

Milwaukeeans of 1896 Paid for Their Amusements

When I was a small child, the Fourth of July always meant Jackson Park. We'd begin the day with a doll buggy and coaster wagon parade, which invariably ended in a line for free ice cream. The afternoon's speeches and songs made no lasting impression, but I have clear memories of the evening fireworks. There were four of us under the age of eight at one point, and the display inspired the familiar blend of sharp excitement and sheer terror. My parents generally had us watch from the safety of our backyard on S. Thirty-fourth Street.

In a case of continuity that seems entirely too rare, the Fourth of July still means Jackson Park. Thousands of Milwaukeeans still gather at Jackson and other local parks for the same attractions I remember from the 1950s: buggies and bicycles festooned with crepe paper; free ice cream; talent contests; and wide-eyed children gazing heavenward as the sky explodes with color and sound.

The tradition of free public entertainment on the Fourth of July seems as old as the city itself, but Milwaukeeans of the 1890s would find our traditions remarkable. They observed the nation's birthday with at least as much vigor as modern citizens, but they did so privately, and they generally paid for the privilege.

There weren't many alternatives at the turn of the last century, simply because Milwaukee's park system was still in its infancy. What the city had, and had in abundance, was an assortment of private beer gardens and picnic groves. On July 4, 1896, despite overcast skies and periods of light rain, all were thronged with admission-paying patriots who gathered for activities ranging from formal balls to "sham battles" fought by uniformed soldiers.

Milwaukeeans could choose from a number of other attractions. The newest was "Shoot the Chutes," a ride that made its debut on July 4, 1896. For one thin dime—roughly two dollars in today's coin—brave souls could climb aboard a "water toboggan" on the east bank of the Milwaukee River and plunge into the stream just above the North

Avenue dam. "It is adventuresome enough to make it fascinating to young people," reported the *Milwaukee Sentinel*, "and there is an additional delight in the irresistible impulse with which the young man's sweetheart clings to his shoulder just before the plunge."

Those with a quarter to spare might have used it for admission to Schlitz Park, a popular beer garden near Eighth and Walnut Streets. Heading the bill on July 4, 1896, was Dr. Carver's Water Carnival, a show built around two horses, Cupid and Powder Face, who dove forty feet into a tank of water. Nearly 11,000 people turned out to witness the equestrian spectacle. Horses were also the main attraction at one of the day's most expensive events. For one dollar—nearly twenty-two dollars in modern currency—racing fans could watch the region's fastest horses compete in the Independence Handicap at State Fair Park. With a purse of $1,000 in the balance, the steeds raced around an early version of the oval that now features Indianapolis 500 cars.

Milwaukeeans on tighter budgets found their way to a variety of free sporting events. The Cream City Wheelmen held their first-ever bicycle road race over a twelve-mile course that ran from Twenty-eighth and Vliet Streets to Wauwatosa and back again. Nearly 8,000 spectators were on hand to see Edward Rosenberg, a fifteen-year-old riding his brother's bike, take the gold medal. Sailing enthusiasts crowded Juneau Park to watch the Milwaukee Yacht Club's third annual regatta. Their view, unfortunately, was obscured by fog, but the crowds lingered on the bluff until the evening hours.

Other Milwaukeeans were discovering the delights of their new parks. Nearly 3,000 turned out for a free concert sponsored by the streetcar company at Lake Park, and another 2,000 took the company's new line to West (now Washington) Park. Both parcels had been purchased only six years earlier, and neither was completely developed.

No matter how they observed the Fourth of July in 1896, Milwaukeeans did it to the accompaniment of fireworks. July 4th was the only day that pyrotechnics were legal in the city, and residents made the most of their opportunity. The noise level climbed in a steady crescendo through the afternoon hours and reached its peak after sunset, when virtually every beer garden, picnic grove, and private club in the county had its own fireworks display.

The festivities on the Milwaukee River were especially spirited. The river was a far more important recreational resource than the lakefront a century ago, and the banks above the North Avenue dam were lined with beer gardens, canoe clubs, and summer homes. A *Sentinel* reporter described the scene in 1896: "In the evening the banks of the upper Milwaukee river for several miles were ablaze with colored fire and displays of fireworks from the grounds of residences and resorts, lighting the dark surface of the water and the deep shadows along the shores with strangely picturesque effect."

The riverside displays of the 1890s probably couldn't hold a Roman candle to the lakefront fireworks we enjoy today. The explosions are presumably bigger, and so are the crowds. But the image of "colored fire" blazing up and down our principal river has a certain antique charm. Then as now, Milwaukeeans knew how to celebrate.

Milwaukee Mardi Gras flyer

The First Summerfest

Forgotten Monument Recalls Forgotten Celebration

It's not much as civic monuments go—a sixty-foot limestone column topped by a stone ball that seems to represent nothing at all. Despite its prominent location—on the Wisconsin Avenue median near the Central Library—the monument is practically invisible, disguised by its own plainness and overshadowed by the patriotic statuary nearby.

Few Milwaukeeans would even recognize a photo of the shaft, and fewer still have read the inscription at its base: "Presented to the City of Milwaukee by the Carnival Association, June 26, 1900." The association is long forgotten, but its column still stands as a lonesome reminder of a celebration that might be considered our first Summerfest.

The story begins in 1897, when a group of civic leaders noticed that Wisconsin was coming up on its fiftieth anniversary of statehood. Taking Mardi Gras as their inspiration, the group began to plan the most lavish celebration the city had ever known. "Carnival," they called it, and Milwaukee was virtually shut down for a full week between June 27 and July 2, 1898. A Grand Carnival Ball was held in the brand-new Central Library. A monument depicting a Civil War battle charge was dedicated on the Court of Honor at Tenth and Wisconsin. Each day featured a different event: a military parade, an "illuminated bicycle pageant," a floral parade, a historical pageant, and a sailing regatta. There were also continuous band concerts, an encampment of 300 Indians on the lakeshore and, of course, fireworks launched from the new federal breakwater. One line at the bottom of the Carnival program virtually guaranteed healthy attendance: "Everything Free." The celebration was so successful that organizers decided to make it an annual event.

Carnival was made to order for David S. Rose, Milwaukee's new mayor. Nicknamed "All the Time Rosy," he was an irrepressible civic booster who once said, "I love to see my people at play and happy." Rose held the city's top job for ten years between 1898 and 1910, running on a platform of "Conventions, Celebrations and a Live Town." What that meant in practice was a wide-open town. Prostitution, gambling dens, and all-night saloons flourished under Rose, and the mayor took an equally lenient attitude toward bribery, kickbacks, and other forms of civic vice. By the time he stepped down, corruption in Milwaukee had reached its all-time high.

But all that was in the future when Carnival was new. Rose reveled in public celebrations, and Carnival Week was probably the high point of his year. During the festivities of 1900, he appeared at the head of the floral parade in a carriage covered from top to bottom with American Beauty roses. The mayor himself was a picture of sartorial splendor, wearing a black Prince Albert coat, a silk top hat, and gray silk gloves.

Pageants and parades were again the featured events in 1900, but the fun carried over to the sideshows, which included concerts by the Heinegabubler Sauerkraut Capella, a band of twenty-four pieces "with every piece guaranteed to be out of tune." Carnival also offered thrills you won't find on any State Fair midway. On June 29, Milwaukee's firemen showed how easy it was to jump into a life net from a height of fifty feet—an invitation they extended to "any citizens who may wish." The fireworks display for 1900 covered "every device in the line of set and explosive illumination that is capable of making a brilliant and popular effect," including skyrockets and Roman candles, bombs and "flowerpots," as well as ground displays depicting Niagara Falls, a Wisconsin badger, and Dewey's battleships in Manila Bay.

The 1900 Carnival was also a showcase for cutting-edge technologies. The city's first-ever automobile parade took place on June 28, and it included nearly thirty horseless carriages, all of them open-air vehicles powered by steam, electricity, or gasoline. Even more impressive was the electric pageant held on the same evening. Electricity was still a novelty in 1900, and spectators gaped in wonder as a procession of lighted floats made its way down the city's streetcar tracks. Nearly 6,000 colored lights were used to outline the battleship *Wisconsin*, scenes from mythology, Jonah and the whale, and characters from Mother Goose. The result, declared the *Milwaukee Sentinel*, was "the most beautiful night parade ever planned in America."

And then there was the column. Edward Hackett, the Carnival Association's president, expressed his group's desire for a legacy that would outlive "the frivolities and gayeties of the Carnival," a monument that would add "something substantial and ornamental to the artistic features of our city." Their choice was the present limestone column, topped by a five-foot metal eagle. (The bird flew the roost for "safety reasons" in 1942.) Rex, the costumed King of Carnival, presented the monument to the people of Milwaukee on June 26, urging them to view it as a symbol of celebration and a constant reminder of "the many mercies had from relaxation, fun and laughter." Accepting on behalf of the city, David Rose's cup ranneth over. As he surveyed the spectacle around him, the mayor pronounced Milwaukee "the land of plentiousness, of peacefulness, of progressiveness, and above all of the greatest happiness that can come to man upon this terrestrial sphere."

The column spawned a minor mystery that persisted for more than a century. The Carnival Association reportedly buried a time capsule in their monument, and some curious latter-day Milwaukeeans suggested that city officials exhume it in time for the shaft's centennial in 2000. Further research revealed that the organizers had indeed prepared a copper "dedication box," but they placed it under an eighteen-ton capstone that was covered, in turn, by the three stones of the main shaft, each eleven feet tall and weighing eleven tons. The box, in short, lies under more than fifty tons of stone rising more than fifty feet in the air. Nothing but a heavy-duty crane or perhaps an earthquake could dislodge it, and the city had no interest in spending the $30,000 it might cost to take the column apart and put it back together. Our ancestors' priceless documents rest serenely at the heart of the monument, as secure as a pharaoh's mummy.

Fortunately, surviving newspaper accounts provide a fairly complete inventory of the box's contents: the morning and evening papers of the day, the bylaws of the Carnival Association, a Wisconsin Blue Book, the city charter, and a greeting signed by the Carnival board. Most of these items are still readily available across the street in the Central Library. Carnival's organizers, in other words, filled their time capsule with generic materials, hid it in a place where no one could recover it, and then told us what was inside. They will not go down in history as the brightest lights in the municipal firmament.

Whatever their deficiencies as planners, Carnival's leaders did share one trait with their modern counterparts: They knew how to throw a party. For four days in 1900, the city was, in the *Milwaukee Journal's* words, "a blaze of light, of color and of sound, to say nothing of the buzz of humanity, bright, gay and happy humanity."

Milwaukee's Carnival ran for one more year and then folded its tents. The all-volunteer effort apparently ran out of steam, but an important precedent had been set. In 1933, Carnival was reincarnated as the Milwaukee Midsummer Festival, a free lakefront extravaganza that enjoyed an eight-year run. In 1968, the spirit of celebration took more permanent form as Summerfest. Although the Carnivals of 1898–1901 set the tone for both events, all that's left from that time is a limestone column hiding in plain sight on Wisconsin Avenue.

Contestants for the title of Miss Midsummer Festival

Summerfest, 1930s-Style

Depression Spawned the First of Milwaukee's Lakefront Festivals

When the gates of Summerfest swing open every June, revelers renew their annual love affair with power chords, horn solos, and free-flowing beer. Since its debut in 1968, the event has become the largest outdoor music festival in America, drawing more than a million people in its busiest years. Milwaukee may be known for beer and Harley-Davidson, but it's just as famous in some quarters as the home of Summerfest.

The event has also earned its place as the largest and longest-running lakefront festival in Milwaukee's history. It is not, however, the first. That distinction belongs to the Milwaukee Midsummer Festival, an almost-forgotten event that provided welcome diversion for local residents at a time when there wasn't much to celebrate.

In 1933, one of the hardest years of the Depression, the Elks Club held its national convention in Milwaukee. Chauncey Yockey, a blue-blooded local lawyer and "exalted ruler" of Milwaukee's Elks, decided to mount a "civic homecoming celebration" in connection with the gathering. Yockey and a host of volunteers organized a week-long series of events for the entertainment of their fellow Milwaukeeans as well as their brother Elks. Most of the festivities were at the lakefront, including boat races, band concerts, carnival rides, and a "Bavarian beer garden" that was usually filled to capacity.

The lakefront activities had one overpowering draw: free admission. Milwaukee has always had a well-deserved reputation for thrift, but thrift was a matter of survival in the 1930s. With unemployment approaching 40 percent, entertainment-starved Milwaukeeans found the free homecoming celebration irresistible. Attendance for the week topped 500,000, and there was growing demand to make the event an annual affair.

The result was the Midsummer Festival, a civic celebration staged every year from 1934 through 1941. The event generally lasted for a full week in mid-July, and its home was a half-mile stretch of lakefront between the Juneau Park lagoon and the north end of today's Summerfest grounds. The War Memorial Center and the Milwaukee Art Museum's Calatrava addition lie near the center of the grounds.

Like Summerfest, the Midsummer Festival offered something for everyone. Organizers highlighted themes that seem to be indelibly stamped on Milwaukee's character—ethnic heritage, for one. The Festival of Many Nations, a forerunner of today's ethnic festivals, was among the event's high points. Dozens of groups, from the Armenians to the Welsh, performed in native costumes for their neighbors. The emphasis was heavily European, but the Festival was, for its time, admirably inclusive. In 1936, for instance, the United Choirs of the Colored Churches of Milwaukee helped open the celebration, and one of the Festival's mainstays was an "authentic" Indian Village erected every year by Potawatomi and Ojibwe tribal members from northern Wisconsin.

Like Summerfest, the Midsummer Festival gave patrons their fill of beer, carnival rides and, of course, music. Major stars like Benny Goodman and Hoagy Carmichael never made it to the lakefront, simply because the Festival couldn't afford them. Pledged to a free-admission policy, organizers depended on the goodwill of local performers and the cooperation of public agencies, including the WPA work relief program. In place of swing bands, the musical attractions included light opera (particularly Gilbert and Sullivan works), an all-state high school band, and a seventy-five-piece accordion orchestra.

Theatergoers were not forgotten. A local troupe staged *As You Like It, The Tempest,* and other Shakespearean classics in the Playhouse on the Green, a temporary stage set against the Juneau Park seawall. The sight of the moon rising behind Prospero and Miranda must have been unforgettable.

And there were fireworks, many with a local touch. Ground displays depicted the Third Ward Fire of 1892; the Return of Beer in 1933; and the Sinking of the *Lady Elgin,* a Lake Michigan steamer that went down in 1860. In 1938, one mile of the breakwater was illuminated with flares and Roman candles. Ten tons of fireworks went up in a typical week, providing "the very last word in modern evening entertainment." Milwaukee's modern obsession with booms and bangs is nothing new.

Fireworks are still familiar, but today's Summerfest patrons might find some features of the Midsummer Festivals a little strange: motorcycle hill climbs above Bradford Beach, swimming races in the frigid lake waters (including an event for dogs), and exhibitions of "group and solo clubswinging" by the Milwaukee Turners. But the most unusual attraction, by modern standards, was undoubtedly the annual pageant. The Festival pageants usually dramatized, with dubious accuracy, historical events like the coming of Solomon Juneau and the Bridge War of 1845.

The producers (most of them WPA relief workers) aspired to even greater heights in 1937. The pageant's centerpiece that year was a "symbolic nature wedding" of the land and Lake Michigan. The "bride" approached by water, escorted by Father Neptune and four attendants representing the other Great Lakes. The "groom" approached by land, flanked by attendants representing the Fields, the Forests, the Mountains, and the Snows. The nuptials took place on a lakefront platform, where the happy couple was surrounded by "a host of girls and women dressed in white and blue, whose movements simulate the shoreline."

The symbolism of the pageants was a bit heavy-handed at times, but the Midsummer Festival's larger civic symbolism was unmistakable. In 1939, Mayor Daniel Hoan described the gathered throngs as "one large, happy family, playing together as we work together for the greater glory of the city we all love." Carl Zeidler, who defeated Hoan in 1940, stressed the promotional aspects of the Festival, calling it "the greatest singly agency we have to promote good will in the state and nation." The 1940 Festival included a drawing for out-of-town visitors. Nearly 7,500 registered, and a surprised Virginian won a grand piano. How he got it home is unrecorded.

Carl Zeidler was, among other things, an irrepressible baritone, and he worked the Festival crowds tirelessly. In 1940, the Potawatomi of the Indian Village adopted the mayor and renamed him Man-Wah-Tuck, "He with the Golden Voice." After welcoming the Indians to "the city of high buildings," Zeidler obligingly donned a headdress, climbed atop the nearest drum, and belted out *God Bless America*.

The Midsummer Festival continued to draw crowds even as the clouds of the Depression lifted; attendance topped out at 1,245,000 in 1940. Crowd estimates for free events are notoriously generous, but Summerfest has yet to reach the same peak.

Although its popularity was self-evident, the Midsummer Festival was, in the end, a casualty of World War II. Five months after the 1941 spectacle, America entered the fray, and the event quickly became a memory. But a seed had been sown. In 1939, Dan Hoan expressed hope that the Midsummer Festival "in time will become recognized as a national institution," every bit as famous as Mardi Gras and the Kentucky Derby. That hope died during the war, but it was revived by Mayor Henry Maier in the 1960s. The seed sprouted again as Summerfest in 1968. Minus the ponderous pageants and the grand pianos, we've been enjoying it ever since.

Centurama

The Milwaukee Centurama of 1946

City Celebrated 100 in Style

It was not, in retrospect, the best year to celebrate a civic birthday. World War II had just ended, servicemen were still coming home, and residents faced a critical housing shortage. But 1946 marked the centennial of Milwaukee's cityhood, and local leaders decided to celebrate it anyway. The show they put on may have been the most ambitious civic commemoration on one site in Wisconsin's history.

Planning had begun much earlier. In 1940, six years before the occasion, Mayor Carl Zeidler used his first and only inaugural address to call for a civic blow-out. "The city's hundredth birthday," he said, "should be observed in such a brilliant style that the eyes of the nation will be upon us." What the mayor envisioned was a sort of home-grown World's Fair put on by what he called "the biggest small town in the country."

Pearl Harbor pushed Zeidler's plans to the back burner. By the time the war ended, he had perished at sea while serving in the Navy, and nearly 200,000 defense workers had made Milwaukee a major center of military production. With the return of peacetime in 1945, planning resumed in earnest. Although some advised waiting for the state's centennial in 1948, Milwaukee's leaders decreed that, after fifteen years of depression and war, their city was ready for a party.

The result was the Centurama, a mid-summer extravaganza that covered the lakefront from the harbor mouth to the Juneau Park lagoon. For an entire month, from July 12 through August 11, 1946, Milwaukee's shoreline came alive with plays, pageants, concerts, air shows, military exhibits, water ballets, a carnival midway, and thirty-one consecutive nights of fireworks. The Centurama was billed as "the Largest City Celebration in the Nation," and organizers blithely predicted attendance of three million.

Milwaukeeans did flock to the lakefront in record numbers. Some came to see national headliners like Eddie Cantor and the now-forgotten dance team of Veloz and Yolanda. Others turned out for the nightly historical pageant, which featured a cast of 450 in full costume. Still others came to see "football fundamentals" demonstrated by the Green Bay Packers or military curiosities like Hermann Goering's field car.

Some Centurama patrons were shocked by the prices they found on the grounds. Front-row seats in the temporary lakefront theater cost $3.60—nearly $35 in today's dollars. Hundreds of characteristically frugal Milwaukeeans chose to watch the stage shows through cracks in the fence or from the bridge on Lincoln Memorial Drive. There was also general agreement that concessionaires were charging too much. The *Milwaukee Journal* lodged a classic complaint: "Twenty cents for a hot dog is gouging in any man's language." Prices on the midway were so high that the county board forced operators to cut them in half before 6 P.M.

A series of misadventures attracted more bad publicity. Traffic on the midway plummeted when a random health check turned up fifteen carnival workers with syphilis or tuberculosis. Attendance at the midday matinee, reserved for shows put on by smaller Wisconsin cities, was so anemic that Beaver Dam, Janesville, and Marshfield canceled their presentations. A Navy demolition team, upset that their underwater charges had fizzled one day, went overboard the next. They set off 3,000 pounds of explosives outside the breakwater, breaking windows and bringing down plaster all over the East Side.

Despite these small-scale disasters, there were some memorable high points during the Centurama's long run. When movie stars Dennis Morgan and Jack Carson came to town for the premiere of *Two Guys from Milwaukee* on July 25, they were mobbed by 100,000 adoring fans, most of them described as "bobby socksers." Reversing the usual roles, the stars appeared at the Centurama to present Mayor John Bohn with the key to Warner Brothers Studios.

On the same day, an intrepid military pilot put his P-80 Shooting Star through its paces over the lakefront. After warming up with a few practice loops and spins, he skimmed twenty feet above the water at the breathtaking speed of 605 miles per hour. The pilot's name was Chuck Yeager.

The Centurama also provided a showcase for Milwaukee's vaunted ethnic diversity. Nearly 2,000 costumed citizens marched in a "panorama of nationalities" during the main parade on July 14. Two weeks later, a thousand-voice chorus performed on the Centurama stage, with singers from the Baeden Maennerchor, the Lapham Park Jewish Chorus, and the Milwaukee Urban League.

The spectacle finally ended on August 11. Attendance fell just short of the three million estimate, and the books closed with a deficit of $41,000 (on a total budget of $388,000). The final reviews were mixed. There was a general consensus that the planning process had been too short, the event too long, and the budget too small. "The Centurama was good in some respects," summarized the *Milwaukee Journal*, "but it was not sufficiently good all the way through to commemorate properly the one hundredth birthday of the state's metropolis." Other participants were less guarded in their comments. Mayor Bohn described the event as "the spectacle of the century," and Eddie Cantor called Milwaukee "the most civic minded city that I have ever played in."

Whatever its shortcomings, the Centurama set a new standard for civic celebrations in Wisconsin. They had just fought a war, but residents of the state's largest city were determined to proclaim their hometown pride. You have only one chance to celebrate a century, they realized. For an entire month, Milwaukee made the most of its opportunity.

Wisconsin State Fair Poster, 1900

Where City Meets Country
State Fair Is Wisconsin's Common Ground

Heaven, I've always thought, must be a slightly enlarged version of the Wisconsin Products Pavilion. Every year at State Fair time, my thoughts turn to that oasis near the center of the grounds, that inexhaustible source of every good thing from the farms and fields of our state: baked potatoes, caramel apples, cherry sundaes, chocolate milk, cheddar cheese, basswood honey, cranberry tarts, maple candy, and so much more. At the height of summer, when I'm hiking in the backwoods or biking on the back roads, just the thought of that garden of culinary delights is enough to make my mouth water and my eyes glaze over with longing.

The Wisconsin Products Pavilion—Ag Products in an earlier time and a different building—has always been a high point of my family's annual visits to the fair. My children, I know, have vivid memories of enjoying potatoes slathered with butter and sour cream while they sat on the strawbales outside the building.

Like so many other Wisconsinites, I have vivid State Fair memories of my own, but not all are so pleasant. As a little kid in the 1950s, I was scared witless by a huge papier-mâché likeness of Alice in Dairyland, a homemade goddess who could roll her eyes, move her arms, and even talk. One year, she singled out my sister in the crowd, and the experience rattled all of us. Many years later, when I saw the cult classic *The Attack of the 50-foot Woman*, my thoughts shot back instantly to that enormous Alice at Fair Park.

Every generation has its own immutable memories, but the history of the Wisconsin State Fair is a chronicle of change. In its earliest years, the fair had no fixed home, no permanent program, and no shortage of financial problems. The park's current incarnation is only the latest in a long procession that goes back to the first years of statehood. The annual spectacle began as a "Cattle Show and Fair" held in Janesville in 1851—just three years after Wisconsin joined the Union. Sponsored by the State Agricultural Society, its purpose was to recognize outstanding farmers and to encourage others to emulate them. The first fair's events included a quarter-acre plowing match and the showing of a 200-pound squash.

The annual exhibition led a nomadic existence for more than forty years, shuttling between Janesville, Milwaukee, Watertown, Madison, and Fond du Lac. In 1891, tired of the constant motion and the chronic financial woes, the Agricultural Society decided to guarantee strong attendance by planting their event in the state's population center. The first fair on the present West Allis grounds was held in 1892.

Although agriculture remained its primary focus, the State Fair offered any number of other attractions. A dog-powered butter churn was displayed in 1900. A locomotive collision was the grandstand feature in 1902, foreshadowing the demolition derbies of more recent times. In 1909, sculptors fashioned a bust of President Taft from Wisconsin butter, and, in 1913, a group of fearless motorists played an exhibition match of "auto polo."

Over the years, the fair developed an assortment of semi-permanent features: horse racing (of the trotter variety) on a dirt track, an amusement park with its own carousel and Tunnel of Love, and the Modernistic Ballroom. More familiar attractions appeared later in the twentieth century. In 1924, Wisconsin's bakers sold their first cream puff, and in 1939 the Green Bay Packers beat the New York Giants in the NFL championship game played on the race track's infield. One year later, sixty dairy queens were honored at a Dairy Ball in the Modernistic Ballroom.

Over the course of a century, State Fair Park became a self-contained world of contrasting sights and sensations. Some fairgoers gravitated to the aromatic clutter of the food concessions. Others sought out the animals, from the bedlam of the poultry building to the contented calm of the dairy barns. Still others appreciated the breathing space of the leafy DNR grounds, the bark and brawl of the midway, or the endearing tackiness of the commercial exhibits. (My family has brought home its share of laser knives, chamois cloths, and hammock chairs.) From carnival hands to cattle judges, from horse pulls to taffy pulls, the Wisconsin State Fair became a showcase for grassroots America at its most genuine.

The key constant in the fair's long history has been its role as a bridge between Milwaukee and the rest of Wisconsin. With the possible exception of the grocery store, no place in the state serves more admirably as an intersection of city and country. Milwaukeeans realize they are Wisconsinites during the fair, and residents of outlying counties have a chance to absorb the textures of their state's metropolis. State Fair Park will continue to change, as it has since the beginning, but I have no doubt that the bridge between city and country will hold, and that my own slice of heaven, Wisconsin-style, will still occupy a place of honor.

Winter

Shoveling snow in Milwaukee, 1925

Milwaukee family, 1866

Winter at the Edge of the World
Milwaukee's Pioneers Spent Months in the Deep Freeze

"By January it had always been winter," wrote E. Annie Proulx in *The Shipping News*. Her novel was set in Newfoundland, but Proulx's observation translates easily to Wisconsin. Every winter, even the occasional mild one, seems to last forever. By the beginning of March, we begin to doubt that the air was ever warm, that our yards were ever green.

But we've got it easy. Imagine, if you can, what winter was like for the pioneers trying to plant a city here in the 1830s. Lake Michigan was their major link with the outside world. When ice brought shipping to a halt in November, Milwaukee was beyond the reach of civilization until the following April. News was scarce, mail service was exceedingly slow, and the settlers—roughly 1,000 of them by 1837—had only each other to stare at for the next four or five months.

For Solomon Juneau, the veteran fur trader who made a graceful transition to real estate, winter in the woods was business as usual. His new neighbors, most of them from New York and New England, found the experience unsettling. It required, first of all, as much preparation as a polar expedition. In 1836, Albert Fowler listed the provisions he had put aside before the last ship left in November: "four barrels of flour, 100 pounds of butter, a barrel of crackers, a barrel of beef, and a large supply of potatoes, carrots and other vegetables."

A monotonous diet wasn't the only hazard of a frontier winter. Most of the Yankees were young men on the move, and months of enforced idleness must have been maddening. Farmers couldn't farm, developers couldn't develop, and there were very few distractions: no libraries, no televisions, and no DVD players. It was probably a pioneer who coined the term "cabin fever."

There were compensations as well. Some settlers kept their hands in one of the euchre games constantly in progress at the American House and other hotels. Some used the time to study their law books or dig into the latest James Fenimore Cooper novel. Despite the presence

271

of a strong temperance faction, most drank. Pioneer historian James Buck counted more than 100 "rum holes" in frontier Milwaukee, each offering its own brand of warmth and dissipation.

Hardier souls spent much of the season on the ice. The heart of Milwaukee's present downtown was a marsh that provided excellent ice-skating. Benjamin Miller, an 1839 arrival, recalled the central wetlands as a winter wonderland. "I have put on my skates at the corner of Wisconsin and Van Buren streets," he recalled in 1898, "and skated from there south to the old harbor mouth"—a distance of nearly two miles.

The Milwaukee River itself was a major thoroughfare in winter. Increase Lapham, the city's pioneer scientist, described the river in an 1836 letter to his brother: "Sleighs, cutters and jumpers are flying about in every direction. The river is frozen solid as a rock, affording the most smooth and level road imaginable." The stretch between Juneau Avenue and Water Street served as a makeshift race course for Milwaukee's fastest horses.

A pair of New Yorkers, Elisha and Benjamin Edgerton, favored indoor entertainment. In 1836, despite a critical shortage of women, they recruited a Chicago fiddler, Joe Davlin, and paid him $150 to play for a series of winter "cotillion parties." Elisha Edgerton pronounced the cotillions "a great success," and Davlin liked Milwaukee so much that he settled here.

Navigation never resumed before the end of March, and the ice sometimes lasted into early May. By that time, Milwaukeeans must have felt as cut off from the world as a submarine crew. They were ready for new faces, new goods, and newer news. The first ship of the season brought all that and more. It meant the resumption of life.

Winter on the frontier was the human equivalent of hibernation, a time when normal concerns hung in suspended animation. We have largely conquered the season. Moving from home to car to work or school, we travel from one artificial hothouse to another. By March, however, we are as hungry for real warmth and real light as our pioneer ancestors must have been.

When you begin to feel that it's always been winter, take heart. The days lengthen.

CAPT. THOS. G. ANDERSON.

Captain Thomas Anderson

ᴀ Feast of Christmas Past

The Main Course Was Raccoon 200 Years Ago

Between the peak colors of fall and the icy depths of winter, Wisconsinites know a fifth season; one that lasts from late November through early January. I describe it as the Season of Too Much Food. No sooner have we stuffed the Thanksgiving turkey than we're making plans for holiday hams and roast geese—not to mention strategic stockpiles of Christmas cookies. For residents of every background, the holidays are a time of traditional plenty.

Feasting, not surprisingly, is one of Milwaukee's oldest traditions. The abundance of natural resources near the lakeshore supported an Indian settlement of some importance. At least seven villages developed within a mile or two of our present downtown, their residents thriving on whitefish and trout from the rivers, deer and bear from the upland forests, and wild rice from the Menomonee marsh. ("Menomonee," in fact, means "wild rice.") The native tribes, including the Potawatomi, were also avid gardeners. Hundreds of acres within the present borders of Milwaukee County were used to grow corn, beans, pumpkins, and squash. It's safe to assume that there were some memorable feasts when the crops were harvested each fall.

The harvest feasts were long over by early December, and most of the Indians had scattered to their winter hunting grounds. As Christmas approached, the celebrating was left to a ragtag band of fur traders who were spending the cold months here as early as the late 1600s. Milwaukee's first recorded holiday feast—or the first attempt at one—dates from Christmas of 1803. The recorder, Thomas Anderson, was a British Canadian who spent more than fifty years on the upper Great Lakes, first as a fur trader and then as an Indian agent.

At the age of twenty, Anderson had left the comforts of his parents' home in Cornwall, Ontario, for the rigors and romance of the wilderness. Those rigors, the young man soon discovered, included a monotonous diet. On the month-long canoe trip from Montreal to Mackinac Island, Anderson and his men subsisted almost entirely on pea soup.

Writing as delicately as he could, the trader described the "atmosphere" hovering about the canoe, one that "so affected the nasal organs that the men suffered intensely the first few days."

Safely landed on Mackinac—the regional capital of the fur trade—Anderson was desperate for home cooking. Remembering the frycakes his mother had made when he was a boy, the sojourner mixed flour with a little water and salt, cut the dough into animal shapes, and dropped them, one by one, into a kettle of hot "tallow"—animal fat. The cakes were soon so nicely browned, Anderson recalled, that his mouth "fairly watered to overflowing." Appearances were deceptive: "On their touching the cold plates, to my horror, . . . the tallow became as hard as a candle." His frycakes were "tough as sole leather," forcing Anderson back to a diet of pea soup and corn chowder.

Later in his career as a trader, Thomas Anderson discovered another backwoods treat that was something less than heart-healthy: venison fried in deer fat. The results were again disappointing: "These steaks I could not eat hot enough to prevent their congealing in their progress to my throat; consequently the roof of my mouth would become so thickly cased over with tallow as to necessitate the use of my knife to remove it."

Anderson was clearly a bungler in the kitchen, but he tried again during his first winter in Milwaukee. Arriving near the end of 1803, he opened a trading post near what is now Jones Island. Two French Canadians, Antoine Le Clair and Alexis Lafromboise, were trading in the vicinity, but they welcomed their newest competitor. Determined to repay their hospitality, Anderson invited his neighbors to a Christmas Day feast in his three-room cabin. For the main course, he chose "the fattest raccoon the Indians could tree"—a ring-tailed giant that weighed thirty-two pounds. The aspiring chef pounded pepper into its skin, stuffed its carcass with chopped venison, and added onions and cedar leaves for seasoning. "No coonship's body," he bragged, "was ever so cram-full before."

The coon was trussed up and ready for the spit by eight o'clock on Christmas Eve. "Then where should it be placed for safety during the night to prevent it from freezing? Of course by the fire." Anderson went to bed with visions of the feast to come dancing in his head. Placing his prized roast on the hearth was, it turned out, a disastrous mistake: "But what was my mortification, when I got up at day light to hang my coon up to roast, to find it putrid and stinking! Oh, misery! sympathize with me for my lost labor, and with my friends for their lost dinner."

The spoiled raccoon ended Anderson's culinary career, but he apparently found enough to eat that Christmas—and for the rest of his life in the wilderness. The veteran finally retired to his native Ontario, where he died in 1875 at the age of ninety-five.

There have been countless early-winter feasts in the 200 years since Thomas Anderson's botched banquet. They have marked holidays and holy days, but they are a response, I suspect, to a much older instinct. As solstice passes and the Season of Too Much Food continues, we emulate our ancestors in every northern clime: putting on pounds against the growing cold and the gathering darkness.

Schuster's Christmas Parade

When Reindeer Rode the Rails
Remembering Schuster's Christmas Parade

Reach into Milwaukee's grab bag of Christmas memories. You'll pull out any number of family stories: the smell of kielbasa filling the house after midnight Mass, the sight of a new train set beneath the tree, or even Uncle Frank falling asleep on his mashed potatoes. But the plum, for many, will be the Schuster's Christmas Parade. For Milwaukeeans born in the 1950s and earlier, the parade was a defining feature of the holiday season.

Schuster's Department Stores were a Milwaukee mainstay long before the first Christmas floats rolled out in 1927. The chain's founder was Edward Schuster, a German-Jewish immigrant who settled here in 1882. He established a dry goods emporium on N. Third Street (now Martin Luther King Drive) in 1884 and soon opened two more branches on the North Side, all of them relatively modest shops.

When Edward Schuster died in 1904, Albert Friedmann, the founder's son-in-law, took over the business. Friedmann began a non-stop building program that made Schuster's the premier department store chain in the region. By 1915, shoppers had their choice of three modern, multi-story establishments: Third and Garfield, Twelfth and Vliet, and Eleventh and Mitchell. "Meet me down by Schuster's," Milwaukeeans began to say, and a few added, "where the streetcar bends the corner around."

In 1927, Albert Friedmann launched the parade that would make his stores synonymous with Christmas. It was a spectacle that has no modern counterparts. For starters, the parade ran on the rails of Milwaukee's streetcar system. In the early days of November, Schuster's crews virtually took over the system's Cold Spring car shops at Fortieth and McKinley. Using electric flatcars as foundations, they built elaborate floats depicting Cinderella, the Three Little Pigs, Peter Rabbit, and other figures of fable and fairy tale. On the Saturday after Thanksgiving, they were ready to roll.

The highlight of every parade was, of course, Santa Claus himself, but the Schuster's version was no ordinary Santa. The sleigh on the old man's flatcar was tethered to six live reindeer tended by "a real Alaskan Eskimo" named Me-Tik. After a series of misadventures, the live animals were replaced with stuffed specimens, but Me-Tik remained a fixture in the parade for years.

The Schuster's Parade was, by definition, a neighborhood event. Milwaukee's downtown has always seemed underdeveloped for a city of our size, and one of the key reasons was the success of competing "downtowns" like Third Street and Mitchell Street. Schuster's managed to become the region's leading department store without the ghost of a presence on Wisconsin Avenue. The parade, accordingly, followed a circuitous, seven-mile route through the heart of residential Milwaukee, passing all three Schuster's locations. *Jingle Bells* played continuously as the cars rolled down the streets.

Although the parade was the main event, one member of the supporting cast became a local legend: Billie the Brownie. In the weeks before Thanksgiving, Santa's "faithful helper and advance agent" charted his boss's journey from the North Pole in daily radio reports. Radio was a new medium in the 1920s (Milwaukee's first station hit the airwaves in 1922), and Billie the Brownie attracted thousands of avid listeners.

Through the hard times of the 1930s, the anxieties of World War II, and the boom of the postwar years, the Schuster's Parade remained the single most popular event of the holiday season; attendance at the 1947 spectacle reached the 300,000 mark. But the parade's days on the rails were numbered. Streetcars were an endangered species as early as the 1920s, and buses and cars finally pushed them to extinction after the war. As the rail system was slowly dismantled, the parade's organizers scrambled to find workable routes. In 1955, they gave up, consigning Santa and his helpers to motorized trucks.

The 1961 Schuster's Parade proved to be the last. Gimbels purchased its venerable competitor in the next year and quickly discontinued the event. The memories that remain are indelible. When longtime Milwaukeeans look back to Christmas Past, visions of Santa, Me-Tik, and Billie the Brownie still dance in their heads.

Woman surrounded by holiday gifts and packages

"Bah, Humbug!" in Old Milwaukee
Our Ancestors Got Tired of Shopping, Too

*e*very year, the lights go up a little earlier. Every year, more people ignore the ghosts and jack-o'-lanterns of Halloween, sail right past the Pilgrims and turkeys of Thanksgiving, and proceed directly to Christmas. The first house on our block is usually decorated in October, even before the leaves come down. The stores, of course, are the worst offenders. I'm usually still wearing a T-shirt when the seasonal aisles in our local Target come alive with fake greenery and blinking lights. Christmas seems to fill an entire quarter of the year, and the day is fast approaching when back-to-school sales will go head to head with holiday specials.

Our ancestors were different, weren't they? Not for them, this obsession with shopping and spending that grips us every holiday season. They kept Christ in Christmas, gathering in reverence around the Nativity scene and shunning the crass commercialism that rules our celebration. Didn't they?

Well, guess again. In a sampling of *Milwaukee Sentinel* Christmas issues from the 1800s, I found some surprising signs of what was to come. Yes, the nineteenth century was less secular and less cynical than the twenty-first; the newspaper carried Yuletide poetry, lengthy sermon excerpts, and detailed stories about the good works being done during the Christmas season. But it was not hard to find the dollar signs hiding in the holly, or the unmistakable signs of holiday stress.

Consider a Christmas editorial from 1846—the same year Milwaukee became a city. The *Sentinel*'s editor began, innocently enough, by invoking the spirit of a Dickens Christmas: "The return of the Holiday season, associated from early childhood with pleasant memories of family gatherings, friendly greetings, and general festivity, seems to diffuse a genial glow throughout the whole community and to stir up in every heart its best and purest feelings."

There followed a baldly promotional listing of stores in the rough-hewn frontier town that offered toys, books, dry goods, groceries, variety wares, and "articles of dress and fancy work." "He must be hard to please, indeed," the editor coaxed, "who cannot find something to his taste in making the round we have indicated. To those who think of buying we say, buy quickly."

Milwaukee's commercial pace quickened perceptibly as the century wore on, and the Christmas rush got more and more hectic. In 1884, the *Sentinel* noticed a transformation in downtown Milwaukee: "There is an epidemic of brown-paper parcels. They form processions on the streets—one sees packages coming and going as he sees bits of green moving everywhere on a Palm Sunday. . . . Indeed, the bundles seem to have possession of the streets and the cars, and the human beings are subordinate and not essential."

The newspaper had particular sympathy for the shopper, typically male, who put off his purchases until the last minute: "All day long he will wander from place to place like a peddler and will find no peace. . . . He is tired, cross, snubbed, and finally despairing. Late in the day he buys something particularly inappropriate at a price far beyond his means and is thoroughly unhappy."

The engine of Christmas commerce was in high gear by the end of the nineteenth century. December issues of the 1898 *Sentinel* were larded with advertisements for all types of gifts. Heyn's store offered willow doll carriages for thirty-three cents and dolls for thirty-nine cents. (These were "J.D. Kestner's celebrated corked and stuffed, kid body, bisque head Dolls," normally priced at sixty-five cents.) Gimbel's advertised 100-piece sets of porcelain dinnerware for $4.98 and sets of Haviland china for less than $8. Espenhain's, another downtown department store, sold "Genuine Mountain Lion Rugs, full head, open mouth, value $35, a handsome present, at $22.50." J.B. Thiery & Co. had "High-Grade Kimball" pianos starting at $265, and Ripple's, on Third Street, promised to "Make Your Feet Merry" with $3 shoes. American Beauty roses, by contrast, sold for the surprisingly modern price of $24 a dozen in 1898. "Worth their weight in gold," claimed the *Sentinel*, reporting a rush of out-of-town orders, "especially from millionaire lumbermen in the Northern woods." (You can multiply by twenty-two to calculate the current dollar values for all these items. Most were still astoundingly cheap, although the roses would have cost well over $500.)

With so much to buy, Christmas festivity turned to Christmas frenzy. December 24, reported the 1898 *Sentinel*, was "a wild carnival time of belated gift-buying." Men were once again the principal offenders. I confess to a hint of familiarity with this description: "Men almost invariably leave their Christmas buying to the last, and then at the eleventh hour rush forth intent only on spending a given sum in a given time. . . . What he wants is to spend his money, as speedily and smoothly as possible." The result, according to the paper, was "many a feminine tear over masculine density of intellect."

But it wasn't just last-minute shoppers who found the commercial crush of Christmas simply too much at times. Male or female, the relentless pressures of the season made some Milwaukeeans want to scream. The *Sentinel* quoted a particularly expressive malcontent in 1898: "Christmas is overdone and overrated. It is a season of reckless extravagance, of entailing obligations on other people and of striving to meet obligations that ought never to have been thrust on one. It's a bore, a stupid farce, and I'm done with it. Not a present shall I make."

No matter how much you love Christmas, have you ever tired of the holiday hoopla? Are there times when you resent the calculated attempts to open our wallets during the season when we open our hearts? Relax—you're carrying on an old Yuletide tradition.

Milwaukee Christmas Tree

O Tannenbaum, Milwaukee-Style

Socialists Put Up City's First Christmas Tree

For most Milwaukeeans, the tradition of a community Christmas tree may seem as old as the city itself. Recent specimens, all of them donated by local residents whose yards they'd outgrown, have risen proudly from the center of Red Arrow Park, directly behind City Hall. Decked out with bright lights and oversized ornaments, they need only snow to complete a postcard picture of Christmas in the city.

Even the oldest traditions have to begin somewhere, and Milwaukee's tree has a somewhat surprising origin. The custom dates to 1910, a year of radical experimentation in local government. Milwaukee was not exactly a model city at the time. Under Mayor David Rose, vice had flourished, corruption was common, and inefficiency was the prevailing standard. It was the Socialists who emerged as the most viable alternative. Led by Victor Berger, a tireless theoretician and master strategist, they became the party of reform. Milwaukee's Socialists fielded their first full slate of candidates in 1898, gathered strength with every election, and finally took the reins of city government in 1910.

At the head of the ticket was Emil Seidel. Milwaukee's new mayor, like most of the city's new alderman, worked with his hands. Seidel was a woodcarver and patternmaker with years of experience in local shops, and he brought the outlook of a skilled craftsman to Milwaukee's top job. "The city government is like a larger machine," he said, and Seidel tried to make it work for everyone.

In a relatively small but entirely characteristic gesture, Emil Seidel also tried to soften the Socialists' public image. The party had a reputation in some circles for irreligion, even atheism—no small concern in a town where the majority of voters were Catholics, Lutherans, and other devout worshipers. The reputation was not entirely undeserved. Some Socialists were freethinkers in the old German mold, individualists who dismissed religion as two parts myth and one part "opiate of the masses." On Christmas Day in 1888, a group of South Side Socialists had attracted the media's attention by decorating a tree with a red flag and exchanging presents to mark the "pagan rite of the sun." Other party faithful organized Socialist Sunday schools that offered lessons in politics rather than Scripture.

Activities like these brought down the wrath of local church authorities. In 1911, more than a year after Seidel's victory, Archbishop Sebastian Messmer minced no words: "Socialism is a heresy and an evil, the viciousness of which is apparent to every thinking man. The immorality which socialism breeds and the dangers which it leads to can only be averted by the influence of religion. . . ."

Emil Seidel was one Socialist who could believe in God and the working class at the same time. Raised in a pious, even pietistic, German Evangelical household, he was not only comfortable with religion but also a celebrated lover of Christmas. It was Seidel who organized his Socialist ward unit's Christmas party every year, an event that featured a tree, carols, and gifts for every child.

It was natural, then, that the mayor would embrace the concept of a community Christmas tree. The actual idea came from a magazine story Seidel happened upon in December 1910. It described a school-teacher who put up a tree in the public square of her small town "to cheer the sojourner who could not be home for Christmas." The story "fired my imagination," Seidel recalled in his memoirs. "Why not a Community tree for Milwaukee? There must be many strangers within our gates who can not be home for Christmas. A tree will make them feel at home."

With no time for formal Common Council approval, Seidel had a tree erected in the Court of Honor, at Ninth Street and Wisconsin Avenue. On Christmas Eve, 1910, the carillon of a nearby church rang out carols, a band played seasonal favorites, and Seidel gave "a Merry Christmas talk." But the star of the show, remembered the mayor, was "Milwaukee's first Community Christmas tree," which "blazed forth in all its glory."

This hastily arranged program set the precedent for what soon became a cherished annual observance. In 1916, the Municipal Christmas Tree Commission was established—a sure sign that the event had arrived. As the tradition evolved, Commission members tried hard to keep it fresh. In 1930, for instance, the Christmas tree was "lighted by radio from an airplane." When natural trees began to seem too small, the Commission decided to build its own. Until the late 1970s, Milwaukee's "tree" was actually a stack of hundreds of smaller evergreens carefully arranged on a wooden frame. The tree also changed addresses more than once, moving from the Court of Honor to MacArthur Square and finally to Red Arrow Park.

What did not change over the decades was the spirit that motivated Emil Seidel in the first place. Many years ago, Milwaukee's first Socialist mayor put up Milwaukee's first community Christmas tree. In the twenty-first century, no less than in 1910, the tree stands as a light in the darkness, reminding all who pass of the promise of the first Christmas: peace on earth, good will to everyone.

Index

Page numbers in italics indicate illustrations.

Index

Index